Financierpro, Publishing
P.O. Box 2266
Antioch, Tn. 37011
enterthecrios@gmail.com
www.financierpro.com

# Table of Contents

# Introduction

Marketing is a term used to describe the process of creating, promoting, and selling a product or service. It involves understanding the target audience, developing a strategy to reach that audience, and implementing that strategy through a variety of channels. At its core, marketing is about identifying customer needs and desires and creating solutions to meet those needs. This involves a deep understanding of the target audience, including their demographics, psychographics, and behaviors. By understanding what motivates and drives the target audience, marketers can create messaging and campaigns that resonate with them. Marketing also involves the creation of a brand identity. A brand is the personality of a product, service, or company. It includes everything from the name and logo to the messaging and packaging. A strong brand identity is essential for creating a connection with the target audience and establishing trust and credibility. Marketing also involves the development of a marketing strategy. This strategy includes a plan for how to reach the target audience and achieve marketing objectives. It includes everything from the selection of marketing channels to the development of messaging and creative assets. Marketing channels can include traditional media, such as television, radio, and print, as well as digital media, such as social media, email, and mobile apps. The selection of marketing channels is based on the target audience and the marketing objectives. Once the marketing strategy has been developed, it is implemented through a variety of tactics. These tactics can include advertising, public relations, direct marketing, and sales promotions. Each tactic is designed to reach the target audience and achieve specific marketing objectives. Marketing also involves measurement and analysis. It is essential to measure the effectiveness of marketing campaigns to determine their impact on the target audience and the overall success of the marketing strategy. This involves tracking metrics such as website traffic, social media engagement, and sales conversion rates. Marketing is a critical component of any business. It is the process of creating and maintaining relationships with customers and stakeholders. Effective marketing can lead to increased sales, brand loyalty, and overall business success. In summary, marketing is the process of creating, promoting, and selling a product or service. It involves understanding the target audience, developing a strategy to reach that audience, and implementing that strategy through a variety of channels. Marketing also involves the creation of a brand identity, the development of a marketing strategy, and the implementation of tactics to achieve marketing objectives. Finally, marketing involves measurement and analysis to determine the effectiveness of marketing campaigns and the overall success of the marketing strategy.

# Chapter 1
# Understand Your Audience

Marketing is a complex field, with countless strategies and tactics that can be used to achieve success. However, there are certain principles and methods that tend to be more effective than others. In this chapter, we will explore the winning method for marketers, which involves understanding your audience, creating valuable content, and measuring and optimizing your efforts. The first step in any successful marketing campaign is understanding your audience. This involves developing a deep understanding of their needs, interests, and pain points, and using this information to create targeted campaigns that resonate with them. To understand your audience, you can use a range of tools and techniques, including surveys, focus groups, and data analysis. By using these methods, you can gain insights into your audience's demographics, interests, and preferences, and use this information to create more effective marketing campaigns. Once you understand your audience, the next step is to create valuable content that resonates with them. This involves creating content that addresses their needs and interests, provides valuable insights and information, and is presented in a format that is easy to consume and engaging.

To create valuable content, you can use a range of formats, including blog posts, infographics, videos, and social media posts. By experimenting with different formats and analyzing the performance of your content, you can determine which formats and topics resonate most with your audience and create more effective campaigns in the future. Finally, to achieve success in marketing, it is essential to measure and optimize your efforts. This involves tracking the performance of your campaigns, analyzing the data, and using this information to make data-driven decisions to improve your results. To measure and optimize your efforts, you can use a range of tools, including Google Analytics, social media analytics, and A/B testing. By using these tools, you can track metrics such as website traffic, engagement, and conversions, and use this information to identify areas for improvement and optimize your campaigns for better results. To see the winning method in action, let's look at an example of a successful marketing campaign.

Suppose you are a clothing retailer targeting millennials. You conduct surveys and focus groups to understand their needs and preferences, and find that they are interested in sustainable fashion, comfortable clothing, and affordable prices. Based on this information, you create a series of blog posts, social media posts, and videos that highlight your commitment to sustainability, showcase your most comfortable clothing lines, and offer discounts and promotions to make your clothing more affordable. You track the performance of your campaigns using Google Analytics and social media analytics and find that your blog posts and videos are generating the most traffic and engagement. You also use A/B testing to optimize your campaigns, testing different headlines and visuals to see which ones perform best. As a result of your efforts, you see a significant increase in website traffic, engagement, and conversions, and achieve your marketing goals of increasing brand awareness and driving sales. The winning method for marketers involves understanding your audience, creating valuable content, and measuring and optimizing your efforts. By following these principles and methods, businesses can create more effective marketing campaigns that resonate with their target audience, increase engagement and conversions, and achieve their marketing goals. Marketing is a critical component of any business. It helps companies to promote their products and services, reach new customers, and build brand awareness. One of the most important benefits of marketing is its ability to build brand awareness. Marketing helps to get the word out about a company's products and services and helps to create a positive image for the brand. Through marketing, companies can establish their brand identity, convey their mission and values, and differentiate themselves from competitors. Brand awareness is essential for any business, as it helps to increase familiarity with a brand and establish trust with potential customers. A strong brand can also help to attract and retain customers over the long-term, as customers are more likely to remain loyal to a brand that they know and trust. Marketing is also critical for reaching new customers. By promoting products and services through various channels, such as social media, email marketing, and paid advertising, companies can attract new customers who may not have been aware of their brand otherwise.

Marketing also helps companies to target specific segments of the population, such as a certain age group or geographic location. By tailoring marketing efforts to these groups, companies can increase the effectiveness of their marketing and reach the customers who are most likely to be interested in their products or services. Marketing is essential for increasing sales. By promoting products and services through various marketing channels, companies can increase demand for their products and services, and ultimately drive sales. Effective marketing can also help to create a sense of urgency among potential customers, encouraging them to act and make a purchase. By using persuasive messaging and calls to action, companies can encourage customers to take the next step in the buying process, such as visiting a website, filling out a form, or making a purchase. Marketing is not just about attracting new customers; it is also critical for building customer loyalty. Through effective marketing, companies can communicate with their customers, build relationships, and provide value beyond the initial sale. By engaging with customers through email marketing, social media, and other channels, companies can create a sense of community around their brand and foster long-term relationships with their customers. This can help to increase customer loyalty and retention, leading to repeat business and positive word-of-mouth referrals. Marketing is essential for staying ahead of competitors. In today's competitive marketplace, companies must constantly innovate and adapt to stay relevant and attract customers. Marketing can help companies to stay top-of-mind with potential customers and differentiate themselves from competitors. By constantly testing and refining marketing strategies, companies can stay ahead of the curve and adapt to changes in the market. This can help to create a sustainable competitive advantage and ensure long-term success. Marketing is a critical component of any business, providing a range of benefits including building brand awareness, reaching new customers, increasing sales, building customer loyalty, and staying ahead of competitors. By investing in effective marketing strategies, businesses can attract and retain customers, increase sales, and build a strong brand that resonates with their target audience. Marketing is a vital part of any business, as it helps to generate interest and awareness for a product or service. One of the most common marketing techniques is the use of advertisements (ads) to promote a product or service. In this chapter, we will explore the benefits and strategies for marketing and using ads in business.

Marketing is an essential part of our daily lives, whether we realize it or not. From the products we buy to the services we use; marketing plays a crucial role in shaping our purchasing decisions and overall experiences. Marketing provides valuable information about products and services. Through advertising, product descriptions, and other marketing materials, companies can inform consumers about the benefits, features, and pricing of their products and services. This information helps consumers make informed purchasing decisions and can help to prevent buyer's remorse or dissatisfaction with a product or service. Marketing helps us find the products we need by making them more accessible and visible. Through various marketing channels, such as social media, online marketplaces, and traditional advertising, companies can promote their products and make them easier to find. This helps consumers save time and effort when searching for products and ensures that they can find what they need when they need it. Marketing plays a significant role in driving the economy and creating jobs. Companies that invest in marketing are more likely to be successful, which leads to increased profits, job creation, and economic growth. By promoting products and services, companies can create demand and stimulate economic activity, which benefits individuals and communities alike. Marketing is essential for building relationships and trust between companies and consumers. Through effective marketing strategies, companies can create a positive image for their brand, establish themselves as thought leaders in their industry, and build relationships with their customers. This can lead to increased loyalty and repeat business, as well as positive word-of-mouth referrals. Marketing drives innovation by creating a competitive marketplace that encourages companies to constantly innovate and improve their products and services. By promoting new and improved products and services, companies can stay ahead of the curve and meet the evolving needs of consumers. This can lead to improved quality of life and greater convenience for consumers, as well as increased profitability for companies. Marketing can also raise awareness for important causes and social issues. Through social media campaigns, advertisements, and other marketing efforts, companies can promote social responsibility and inspire people to act. This can lead to positive change and help to address important issues such as environmental sustainability, social justice, and public health. Marketing can also provide entertainment for consumers. Through creative and engaging advertisements, companies can capture consumers' attention and provide them with a fun and enjoyable experience. This can help to build brand loyalty and create a positive association between the brand and the consumer. Marketing plays a crucial role in our daily lives, providing valuable information, helping us find the products we need, driving the economy, building relationships and trust, driving innovation, raising awareness for important causes, and providing entertainment. Whether we realize it or not, marketing shapes our purchasing decisions and overall experiences, and is an essential part of our daily lives.

# Chapter 2
# Seven Major Factors of Marketing

One of the primary functions of marketing is to build brand awareness. By promoting products and services through various channels, such as social media, email marketing, and paid advertising, companies can increase brand recognition and familiarity among their target audience. This helps to establish a positive brand image and differentiate the company from competitors. Marketing is critical for increasing sales. By promoting products and services through various marketing channels, companies can increase demand for their products and services, ultimately leading to more sales. Effective marketing can also create a sense of urgency among potential customers, encouraging them to act and make a purchase. Marketing is not just about attracting new customers; it is also critical for building customer loyalty. Through effective marketing, companies can communicate with their customers, build relationships, and provide value beyond the initial sale. By engaging with customers through email marketing, social media, and other channels, companies can create a sense of community around their brand and foster long-term relationships with their customers. Marketing is critical for identifying and anticipating customer needs. Through market research, companies can gain valuable insights into customer behavior, preferences, and pain points. This information can be used to develop new products and services that better meet the needs of customers, ultimately leading to increased sales and customer satisfaction. Marketing is also critical for enhancing the customer experience. By promoting products and services through various marketing channels, companies can make it easier for customers to find and purchase what they need. Effective marketing can also provide customers with valuable information, such as product features, pricing, and customer reviews, that can help them make informed purchasing decisions. Marketing can also encourage innovation by creating a competitive marketplace that encourages companies to constantly innovate and improve their products and services. By promoting new and improved products and services, companies can stay ahead of the curve and meet the evolving needs of customers. This can lead to improved quality of life and greater convenience for consumers, as well as increased profitability for companies. Marketing is critical for driving economic growth. By promoting products and services, companies can create demand and stimulate economic activity, leading to job creation, increased profits, and economic growth. Effective marketing can also attract new businesses to an area, further contributing to economic growth and development.

MARKETING PLAYS A CRITICAL role in any business, providing a range of benefits including building brand awareness, increasing sales, building customer loyalty, identifying, and anticipating customer needs, enhancing the customer experience, encouraging innovation, and driving economic growth. By investing in effective marketing strategies, businesses can attract and retain customers, increase sales, and build a strong brand that resonates with their target audience.

### What are the 3 purposes of marketing?

Marketing is a multifaceted field that involves a wide range of strategies and techniques to promote products and services. At its core, marketing has three primary purposes: to inform, to persuade, and to remind. One of the primary purposes of marketing is to inform consumers about products and services. This involves providing valuable information about the features, benefits, and uses of a product or service, as well as its price and availability. By providing this information, companies can educate consumers about their offerings, and help them make informed purchasing decisions. Marketing can also inform consumers about a company's brand, mission, and values. This information helps consumers understand what a company stands for, and why they should choose that company over its competitors. Through various marketing channels, such as advertising, content marketing, and social media, companies can provide valuable information to their target audience, and establish themselves as thought leaders in their industry. Another key purpose of marketing is to persuade consumers to purchase products and services. This involves creating persuasive messaging and calls to action that encourage consumers to act, such as making a purchase or visiting a website. Effective marketing can create a sense of urgency among potential customers and provide them with the motivation they need to take the next step in the buying process. To persuade consumers, companies must understand their needs, wants, and pain points. By tailoring their messaging and marketing efforts to these factors, companies can create persuasive campaigns that resonate with their target audience. Effective persuasion requires a deep understanding of consumer psychology, as well as strong communication and creative skills. The final purpose of marketing is to remind consumers about a company's products and services. This involves creating consistent messaging and branding that reinforces a company's message and identity. By reminding consumers about their offerings, companies can maintain top-of-mind awareness, and stay relevant in the minds of their target audience.

Marketing reminders can take many forms, including email marketing, social media, and retargeting ads. By reaching out to consumers on a regular basis, companies can keep their brand top-of-mind and encourage repeat business and brand loyalty. Marketing serves three primary purposes: to inform, to persuade, and to remind. By providing valuable information about products and services, creating persuasive messaging, and reminding consumers about a company's offerings, marketing helps companies to reach their target audience, increase sales, and build brand loyalty. Effective marketing requires a deep understanding of consumer behavior, as well as strong communication and creative skills. By investing in effective marketing strategies, companies can achieve their marketing goals and build a strong brand that resonates with their target audience. Marketing and Google Ads co-exist by working together to create a comprehensive digital marketing strategy. While marketing encompasses a range of activities, including branding, market research, and customer relationship management, Google Ads is a specific type of online advertising that can help businesses reach their target audience and achieve specific marketing goals. Google Ads allows businesses to display ads on the Google search engine results page (SERP) and other websites within the Google Display Network. These ads can target specific keywords, demographics, and locations, allowing businesses to reach their ideal customer at the right time and place. Marketing and Google Ads can co-exist by working together to achieve specific marketing objectives. For example, a business may use marketing research to identify their target audience and develop a marketing strategy that includes both branding and advertising. They may then use Google Ads to implement their advertising strategy, such as targeting specific keywords that are relevant to their products or services. By working together, marketing and Google Ads can help businesses achieve a range of marketing objectives, including increasing brand awareness, driving website traffic, and generating leads or sales. For example, a business may use Google Ads to target users who are searching for a specific product or service, while also using marketing techniques to build brand awareness and develop relationships with potential customers. Marketing and Google Ads can also co-exist by sharing data and insights. Google Ads provides businesses with a wealth of data on the performance of their ads, including impressions, clicks, and conversions. This data can be used to inform marketing decisions and improve overall marketing performance. Marketing and Google Ads can also work together to create a seamless customer experience. For example, a business may use Google Ads to drive traffic to their website, where they can use marketing techniques to provide a personalized and engaging experience for visitors. By combining advertising and marketing efforts, businesses can create a cohesive and effective digital marketing strategy that delivers real results. Marketing and Google Ads can co-exist by working together to create a comprehensive digital marketing strategy. By combining advertising and marketing techniques, businesses can achieve specific marketing objectives and create a seamless customer experience. The key is to use data and insights to inform decisions and continually optimize marketing and advertising efforts to achieve the best possible results.

# Chapter 3
# The purpose of Google Ads

Ads can provide many benefits for businesses, including a powerful way to increase brand awareness and recognition. By featuring a product or service in an ad, businesses can expose their brand to a wider audience and build recognition over time. Ads can be targeted to specific audiences based on demographics such as age, gender, location, and interests. This allows businesses to reach their ideal customers more effectively and maximize the impact of their marketing efforts. Ads can be a cost-effective way to reach a large audience, particularly when compared to traditional marketing techniques such as print or television ads. With digital ads, businesses can set a budget and only pay for clicks or impressions, making it easy to control costs. Ads can provide measurable results through analytics and tracking tools. This allows businesses to monitor the performance of their ads and adjust their strategy as needed to improve results. Strategies for Marketing and Using Ads in Business - Before creating an ad campaign, it is important to define your target audience. This will help to ensure that your ads are reaching the right people and maximizing the impact of your marketing efforts. Consider factors such as age, gender, location, interests, and buying habits when defining your target audience. Setting a budget for your ad campaign is crucial to ensuring that you are not overspending on marketing. Consider factors such as the size of your audience, the cost per clicks or impression, and the duration of the campaign when setting your budget. There are many different types of ads to choose from, including display ads, search ads, social media ads, and video ads. Consider the nature of your business and the preferences of your target audience when choosing the right ad format for your campaign. The copy and creative used in your ads can make a big difference in their effectiveness. Be sure to create engaging, attention-grabbing copy and creative that will resonate with your target audience and drive action. Once your ad campaign is up and running, it is important to monitor its performance and adjust your strategy as needed.

Use analytics and tracking tools to measure the performance of your ads and adjust your targeting, copy, or creative as needed to improve results. To get the most out of your ad campaigns, there are several best practices to keep in mind: Ads that are simple and easy to understand are often the most effective. Keep your ad copy and creative straightforward and avoid clutter or overly complex messaging. Test different ad formats, copy, and creative to see what works best for your business. Iterate on your ad campaigns over time to improve results and maximize impact.

Consistency is key when it comes to branding and advertising. Ensure that your ads are consistent with your brand messaging and visual identity to build recognition and trust over time. Include a clear call-to-action in your ads to encourage users to act, whether it is clicking through to a website or making a purchase. Ads are a powerful tool for businesses to generate awareness, drive traffic, and increase sales. By following the best practices and strategies outlined in this chapter, businesses can maximize the impact of their ad campaigns and achieve their marketing goals. From defining the target audience to creating engaging ad copy and creative, and monitoring and adjusting the strategy, businesses can use ads to reach their ideal customers and drive action. However, it is important to keep in mind that ads are just one part of a comprehensive marketing strategy. Businesses should also focus on other marketing techniques such as content marketing, social media marketing, and email marketing to build a strong brand and engage with their target audience. Overall, using ads in business can be an effective way to reach a large audience, build brand awareness, and drive sales. By taking a strategic and thoughtful approach to ad campaigns, businesses can achieve their marketing goals and build a strong brand that resonates with their target audience. Google Ads, formerly known as Google AdWords, is a powerful advertising platform that allows businesses to reach their target audience through targeted advertising campaigns. The primary purpose of Google Ads is to help businesses increase website traffic, generate leads, and boost sales. Here are some of the key purposes of Google Ads: One of the primary purposes of Google Ads is to increase website traffic. By targeting specific keywords and demographics, businesses can reach their ideal audience and drive traffic to their website. This can be particularly useful for businesses that are just starting out or have a new website that is not yet ranking well in search engines. Google Ads allows businesses to create highly targeted campaigns that are designed to reach specific audiences. By using a combination of keywords, ad copy, and targeting options, businesses can create ads that are designed to attract the right type of traffic to their website. Another key purpose of Google Ads is to generate leads. By targeting specific keywords and demographics, businesses can reach potential customers who are actively looking for their products or services. This can be particularly useful for businesses that are looking to generate leads quickly or that have a sales team in place to follow up on leads. Google Ads allows businesses to create lead generation campaigns that are designed to capture leads through a variety of methods, such as form submissions or phone calls. By using landing pages and call-to-action buttons, businesses can create a seamless user experience that encourages potential customers to act. A third key purpose of Google Ads is to boost sales. By targeting users who are actively searching for their products or services, businesses can increase the chances of converting website visitors into paying customers. This can be particularly useful for businesses that are looking to increase their online sales or that have a strong e-commerce presence. Google Ads allows businesses to create highly targeted campaigns that are designed to reach users at all stages of the buying cycle. By using a combination of ad copy, targeting options, and remarketing campaigns, businesses can create ads that are designed to convert website visitors into paying customers. Another important purpose of Google Ads is to increase brand awareness. By displaying ads on the Google search engine results page (SERP) and other websites within the Google Display Network, businesses can increase their visibility and reach a wider audience. Google Ads allows businesses to create display campaigns that are designed to increase brand awareness. By using a combination of ad copy, targeting options, and visual elements, businesses can create ads that are designed to grab the attention of potential customers and increase brand recognition. Google Ads is designed to help businesses measure the results of their advertising campaigns. By providing detailed metrics on ad performance, businesses can track their return on investment (ROI) and make data-driven decisions to improve their campaigns. Google Ads also provides businesses with a range of metrics, including impressions, clicks, and conversions. By using this data, businesses can analyze the performance of their campaigns and adjust improve their ROI. The primary purpose of Google Ads is to help businesses reach their target audience, increase website traffic, generate leads, boost sales, increase brand awareness, and measure results. By using a combination of targeting options, ad copy, and visual elements, businesses can create highly effective advertising campaigns that deliver real results. By using the data and insights provided by Google Ads, businesses can continuously improve their campaigns to achieve the best possible ROI. Google Ads is a powerful advertising platform that allows businesses to reach their target audience and achieve their marketing goals. While Google Ads is not strictly necessary for all businesses, it can be a valuable tool for those looking to increase their online visibility, drive website traffic, and boost sales. Here are some of the reasons why Google Ads can be a valuable tool for businesses: One of the main benefits of Google Ads is its ability to target specific audiences. With Google Ads, businesses can create highly targeted campaigns that reach users who are actively searching for their products or services. This can be particularly useful for businesses that have a niche audience or that offer specialized products or services. By using a combination of targeting options, such as keywords, location, and demographics, businesses can ensure that their ads are reaching the right people at the right time. This can increase the chances of converting website visitors into paying customers. Another key benefit of Google Ads is its ability to increase online visibility. By displaying ads on the Google search engine results page (SERP) and other websites within the Google Display Network, businesses can increase their visibility and reach a wider audience.

This increased visibility can help businesses to build brand awareness, generate leads, and increase sales. It can also help businesses to stay competitive in a crowded marketplace, particularly if they are up against larger or more established competitors. Google Ads can also be a cost-effective way to advertise online. With Google Ads, businesses only pay for clicks on their ads, meaning they are not charged for impressions or views. This can be particularly useful for businesses with limited marketing budgets, as they can control their advertising spend and ensure they are getting the most bang for their buck. Additionally, by using a combination of targeting options, businesses can ensure that their ads are reaching users who are most likely to convert, increasing the chances of achieving a positive ROI. Another key benefit of Google Ads is its ability to provide measurable results. With Google Ads, businesses can track the performance of their campaigns in real-time, allowing them to make data-driven decisions to improve their results. Google Ads provides businesses with a range of metrics, including impressions, clicks, and conversions. By using this data, businesses can analyze the performance of their campaigns and adjust improve their ROI. This level of visibility and control can be particularly useful for businesses looking to optimize their marketing efforts and achieve better results. Google Ads is a flexible advertising platform that can be adapted to meet the needs of different businesses. With Google Ads, businesses can create campaigns that are designed to achieve specific marketing objectives, such as increasing website traffic or generating leads. Additionally, Google Ads can be customized to fit different budgets, targeting options, and ad formats. This flexibility can help businesses to create campaigns that are tailored to their unique needs, without breaking the bank. In conclusion, while Google Ads may not be strictly necessary for all businesses, it can be a valuable tool for those looking to increase their online visibility, drive website traffic, and boost sales. With its ability to target specific audiences, increase online visibility, provide cost-effective advertising, deliver measurable results, and offer flexibility, Google Ads can be an essential part of a comprehensive digital marketing strategy.

# Chapter 4
# Why Google Is So Good at Advertising

Google is one of the world's largest and most successful companies, in large part due to its expertise in advertising. But why is Google so good at advertising? There are several key factors that contribute to Google's success in this area. Google's user base is massive, with billions of people using the search engine and other Google products every day. This gives Google a significant advantage when it comes to advertising, as it has access to a vast pool of potential customers. With so many users, Google can offer advertisers a huge audience to target with their ads. This allows advertisers to reach a wide range of people with their message, making it easier to generate leads, drive traffic, and increase sales. Google's targeting capabilities are some of the most advanced in the industry. With tools like Google Ads, businesses can target specific demographics, locations, and interests to ensure their ads are reaching the right people at the right time. Google's targeting capabilities are particularly powerful when it comes to search advertising. With search advertising, businesses can target users who are actively searching for specific keywords or phrases, making it easier to reach people who are interested in their products or services. Google has access to vast amounts of data, which it uses to inform its advertising strategies. By analyzing user behavior and search patterns, Google can identify trends and patterns that help advertisers to create more effective ads. Google's data analytics capabilities are particularly powerful when it comes to retargeting. With retargeting, businesses can target users who have already visited their website or interacted with their ads in the past. By using data analytics to identify these users and target them with relevant ads, businesses can increase the chances of converting them into paying customers. Google's ad formats are highly effective, with a range of options to choose from depending on the advertiser's goals. For example, search ads are designed to appear at the top of search engine results pages, while display ads can be used to target users on a range of websites. Google's ad formats are also highly customizable, allowing advertisers to create ads that are tailored to their specific needs. This can help businesses to create ads that are more engaging and effective, increasing the chances of generating leads and driving sales. Finally, Google's success in advertising can be attributed to its continuous innovation. Google is constantly updating and improving its advertising products, introducing new features and capabilities that make it easier for businesses to reach their target audience. For example, Google has recently introduced Smart Campaigns, which use machine learning to create and optimize ads for businesses. This technology helps businesses to create more effective ads without the need for extensive marketing expertise. Google is so good at advertising because of its massive user base, advanced targeting capabilities, data analytics, highly effective ad formats, and continuous innovation. By leveraging these strengths, Google has become one of the most successful advertising companies in the world, helping businesses of all sizes to reach their target audience and achieve their marketing objectives. Niche domination refers to the process of becoming the go-to provider within a specific market or industry. This can be achieved by creating a strong brand, offering high-quality products or services, and developing a loyal customer base. Google Ads can be an effective tool for achieving niche domination, as it allows businesses to target specific keywords, demographics, and locations to reach their ideal audience. Here are some of the ways in which niche domination and Google Ads can work together: One of the key benefits of Google Ads is its ability to target specific audiences. By using a combination of keywords, demographics, and location targeting, businesses can ensure that their ads are reaching the right people at the right time. For businesses looking to achieve niche domination, this can be particularly useful. By targeting specific keywords and demographics, businesses can ensure that their ads are reaching the people who are most likely to be interested in their products or services. Another key benefit of Google Ads is its ability to increase online visibility. By displaying ads on the Google search engine results page (SERP) and other websites within the Google Display Network, businesses can increase their visibility and reach a wider audience. For businesses looking to achieve niche domination, this increased visibility can be particularly useful. By ensuring that their ads are appearing at the top of the search engine results page, businesses can position themselves as the go-to provider within their specific market or industry. Building brand awareness is a crucial part of achieving niche domination. By creating a strong brand, businesses can position themselves as the leader within their market or industry. Google Ads can be a valuable tool for building brand awareness, particularly when combined with other marketing efforts. By using targeted keywords and demographics, businesses can ensure that their ads are reaching the right people, increasing the chances of creating a lasting impression and building brand loyalty. Another key benefit of Google Ads is its ability to provide measurable results. By tracking metrics such as impressions, clicks, and conversions, businesses can analyze the performance of their campaigns and make data-driven decisions to improve their results. For businesses looking to achieve niche domination, this level of visibility and control can be particularly useful. By using data to inform their advertising and marketing decisions, businesses can optimize their campaigns and ensure they are getting the most bang for their buck. Finally, Google Ads can be a valuable tool for continuous improvement. By testing different ad formats, targeting options, and messaging, businesses can continually improve their campaigns and stay ahead of the competition. For businesses looking to achieve niche domination, this continuous improvement is crucial. By staying ahead of the competition and continually improving their advertising and marketing efforts, businesses can position themselves as the go-to provider within their specific market or industry. Niche domination and Google Ads can work together to help businesses achieve their marketing goals. By using targeted advertising, increasing visibility, building brand awareness, providing measurable results, and continually improving their campaigns, businesses can position themselves as the leader within their market or industry. With its advanced targeting capabilities, flexible ad formats, and measurable results, Google Ads can be an essential tool for achieving niche domination and growing a successful business. While Google Ads offers many benefits, it also has some disadvantages that businesses should consider before investing in the platform. In this chapter, we will explore the advantages and disadvantages of Google Ads. Targeted Advertising: Google Ads allows businesses to target specific audiences by using keywords, demographics, and location targeting. This can help businesses to ensure that their ads are reaching the right people at the right time, increasing the chances of generating leads and driving sales. Measurable Results: Google Ads provides businesses with a range of metrics, including impressions, clicks, and conversions. This allows businesses to track the performance of their campaigns in real-time, making it easier to make data-driven decisions to improve their results. Increased Visibility: By displaying ads on the Google search engine results page (SERP) and other websites within the Google Display Network, businesses can increase their online visibility and reach a wider audience. Cost-Effective Advertising: Google Ads is a cost-effective way to advertise online, as businesses only pay for clicks on their ads. This can be particularly useful for businesses with limited marketing budgets, as they can control their advertising spend and ensure they are getting the most bang for their buck. Flexibility: Google Ads is a flexible advertising platform that can be adapted to meet the needs of different businesses. With Google Ads, businesses can create campaigns that are designed to achieve specific marketing objectives, such as increasing website traffic or generating leads. Disadvantages of Google Ads - Cost: While Google Ads can be a cost-effective way to advertise online, it can also be expensive if not managed properly. Businesses can quickly run up costs if they are not careful about their bidding strategy and targeting options. Complexity: Google Ads can be a complex platform, particularly for businesses with limited marketing expertise. While there are many resources available to help businesses get started with Google Ads, it can still be a daunting task for those who are not familiar with the platform. Competition: With millions of businesses advertising on Google Ads, competition can be fierce. This can make it difficult for businesses to achieve the results they are looking for, particularly if they are up against larger or more established competitors. Click Fraud: Click fraud is a major concern for businesses advertising on Google Ads. Click fraud occurs when a competitor or a bot clicks on a business's ads repeatedly, driving up costs and wasting advertising dollars. Ad Fatigue: Ad fatigue is a common problem in online advertising, particularly if businesses are running the same ads for an extended period. Over time, users may become immune to the ads and stop paying attention, reducing the effectiveness of the campaign. While Google Ads offers many benefits, it also has some disadvantages that businesses should consider before investing in the platform. By carefully managing their campaigns, monitoring costs, and staying ahead of the competition, businesses can use Google Ads to reach their target audience and achieve their marketing goals. However, it is important for businesses to be aware of the potential drawbacks of Google Ads and to take steps to minimize the impact of these challenges.

# Chapter 5
# How to Get People to Buy from You

The world of business has become increasingly digital in recent years, and now more than ever, it is essential to have an online presence if you want your business to succeed. However, simply having a website or social media profile is not enough. You need to attract potential customers to your online platforms and convince them to make a purchase. In this chapter, we will explore some strategies that you can use to get people to your business online and buy. The first step in attracting customers to your business online is to develop a comprehensive digital marketing plan. This plan should outline the strategies that you will use to reach your target audience and convince them to make a purchase. Some common digital marketing strategies include search engine optimization (SEO), pay-per-click advertising (PPC), social media marketing, email marketing, and content marketing. Your digital marketing plan should also include metrics for tracking your success and adjusting your strategies as needed. Search engine optimization (SEO) is the process of optimizing your website so that it ranks higher in search engine results pages (SERPs). When potential customers search for keywords related to your business, you want your website to appear at the top of the search results. To optimize your website for search engines, you need to focus on on-page factors such as title tags, meta descriptions, header tags, and content. You should also ensure that your website is mobile-friendly and loads quickly. Pay-per-click advertising (PPC) is a digital advertising model where advertisers pay each time a user clicks on one of their ads. PPC advertising can be an effective way to attract potential customers to your website, especially if you are targeting specific keywords or demographics. Some popular PPC platforms include Google Ads and Facebook Ads. Social media marketing is another effective way to attract potential customers to your business online. Social media platforms like Facebook, Twitter, and Instagram offer a range of advertising options that allow you to target specific demographics and interests. You can also use social media to engage with your audience, build brand awareness, and promote your products and services. Email marketing is a powerful tool for reaching potential customers and encouraging them to make a purchase. To use email marketing effectively, you need to build an email list of people who have expressed interest in your products or services. You can then use email marketing to send newsletters, promotions, and other content that encourages your subscribers to make a purchase. Offering discounts and promotions is a great way to attract potential customers to your business online. You can offer discounts on specific products or services, provide free shipping, or offer a discount code to new subscribers. By offering discounts and promotions, you can encourage potential customers to make a purchase and become loyal customers. Providing excellent customer service is essential for building a loyal customer base. When customers have a positive experience with your business, they are more likely to make repeat purchases and recommend your business to others. Make sure to respond to customer inquiries and complaints promptly and go above and beyond to ensure that your customers are satisfied with their purchases. Customer reviews and testimonials are a powerful tool for attracting potential customers to your business online. When customers see positive reviews and testimonials from other customers, they are more likely to trust your business and make a purchase. Encourage your satisfied customers to leave reviews on your website and social media profiles and feature these reviews prominently on your website. High-quality images and videos can help to showcase your products and services and encourage potential customers to make a purchase. Make sure to use high-quality, professional images and videos that accurately represent your products or services. Poor quality images or videos can turn off potential customers and make your business appear unprofessional. Consider hiring a professional photographer or videographer to create high-quality visual content for your website and social media profiles. With more and more people accessing the internet on their mobile devices, it is essential to optimize your website for mobile devices. Make sure that your website is mobile-friendly and loads quickly on mobile devices. A mobile-friendly website will make it easier for potential customers to browse your products or services and make a purchase on the go. Retargeting ads are a type of digital advertising that targets users who have previously interacted with your business online. For example, if a user visits your website but does not make a purchase, you can use retargeting ads to display ads to them on other websites or social media platforms. Retargeting ads can be an effective way to remind potential customers about your business and encourage them to make a purchase. Providing detailed product information on your website is essential for helping potential customers make informed purchase decisions. Make sure to include accurate and detailed descriptions of your products or services, as well as images and videos that showcase your products. Providing detailed product information can help to build trust with potential customers and increase the likelihood of a purchase. A hassle-free checkout process is essential for ensuring that potential customers complete their purchase. Make sure that your checkout process is simple and easy to navigate and consider offering multiple payment options to make it as convenient as possible for customers to make a purchase. You can also offer a guest checkout option for customers who do not want to create an account. Live chat and chatbots can be effective tools for providing customer support and answering questions in real-time. Offering live chat or a chatbot can help to improve the customer experience and increase the likelihood of a purchase. Make sure to staff your live chat or chatbot with knowledgeable support staff who can quickly and accurately answer customer inquiries. Finally, it is essential to monitor and analyze your results to determine what is working and what is not. Use analytics tools to track your website traffic, conversion rates, and other key metrics. Use this data to make informed decisions about your digital marketing strategies and adjust as needed to improve your results. Attracting potential customers to your business online and encouraging them to make a purchase requires a comprehensive digital marketing strategy and a focus on providing an excellent customer experience. By optimizing your website for search engines, using digital advertising, leveraging social media marketing, providing detailed product information, and offering a hassle-free checkout process, you can attract potential customers to your business online and increase your sales. Remember to monitor your results and adjust as needed to continually improve your digital marketing efforts.

# Chapter 6
# Growth Plan and Marketing Strategy

Developing a growth plan and strategy for marketing ads is essential for any business looking to bring customers online and encourage them to make a purchase. A growth plan and strategy will outline the steps that your business will take to reach its growth goals, and it will include a marketing plan that outlines the strategies that you will use to attract potential customers and encourage them to buy. In this chapter, we will explore some key steps to developing a growth plan and strategy for marketing ads. The first step in developing a growth plan and strategy for marketing ads is to define your growth goals. What are you trying to achieve? Do you want to increase sales, expand into new markets, or build brand awareness? Your growth goals will determine the strategies that you use and the metrics that you track. To develop a growth plan and strategy for marketing ads, you need to have a clear understanding of your target market. Who are your ideal customers? What are their needs, interests, and pain points? How do they use the internet, and where do they spend their time online? Analyzing your target market will help you to develop effective advertising strategies that reach the right audience. Once you have defined your growth goals and analyzed your target market, it is time to develop a marketing plan. Your marketing plan should outline the strategies that you will use to attract potential customers and encourage them to make a purchase. Some common marketing strategies include search engine optimization (SEO), pay-per-click (PPC) advertising, social media marketing, email marketing, and content marketing. Search engine optimization (SEO) is the process of optimizing your website and online content so that it ranks higher in search engine results pages (SERPs). By optimizing your website for search engines, you can attract potential customers who are searching for keywords related to your products or services. Some key SEO strategies include using relevant keywords in your content, optimizing your website for mobile devices, and building high-quality backlinks to your website. Pay-per-click

(PPC) advertising is a digital advertising model where advertisers pay each time a user clicks on one of their ads. PPC advertising can be an effective way to attract potential customers to your website, especially if you are targeting specific keywords or demographics. Some popular PPC platforms include Google Ads, Bing Ads, and Facebook Ads. Social media marketing is another effective way to attract potential customers to your business online. Social media platforms like Facebook, Twitter, and Instagram offer a range of advertising options that allow you to target specific demographics and interests. You can also use social media to engage with your audience, build brand awareness, and promote your products and services. Email marketing is a powerful tool for reaching potential customers and encouraging them to make a purchase. To use email marketing effectively, you need to build an email list of people who have expressed interest in your products or services. You can then use email marketing to send newsletters, promotions, and other content that encourages your subscribers to make a purchase. Developing high-quality content is essential for attracting potential customers to your website and building brand awareness. High-quality content can also help to establish your business as an authority in your industry. Some examples of high-quality content include blog posts, infographics, videos, and whitepapers. Retargeting ads are a type of digital advertising that targets users who have previously interacted with your business online. For example, if a user visits your website but does not make a purchase, you can use retargeting ads to display ads to them on other websites or social media platforms. Retargeting ads can be an effective way to remind potential customers about your business and encourage them to make a purchase. By targeting users who have already shown an interest in your products or services, retargeting ads can help you to increase conversion rates and improve the return on investment (ROI) of your advertising campaigns. To ensure that your growth plan and marketing strategies are effective, it is essential to track your results and make data-driven decisions. Use analytics tools to monitor your website traffic, conversion rates, and other key metrics. Use this data to identify areas where you can improve your advertising campaigns and adjust as needed. Monitoring your competition is also essential for developing a successful growth plan and marketing strategy. Keep an eye on what your competitors are doing and use this information to identify areas where you can differentiate your business and improve your marketing efforts.

Look for gaps in the market that your competitors are not addressing and develop advertising campaigns that target these areas. To ensure that your advertising campaigns are effective, it is important to test and optimize them on an ongoing basis. A/B testing is a common technique used in digital advertising to test different versions of an ad to see which performs better. By testing different ad copy, images, and calls to action, you can optimize your advertising campaigns to improve performance and increase conversions. Personalizing your advertising can help to improve the effectiveness of your campaigns and increase customer engagement. Use customer data to create targeted advertising campaigns that are tailored to the interests and needs of your audience. For example, you can use customer data to personalize the content of your emails, or to create targeted ads based on the products or services that a customer has previously purchased. While attracting new customers is important, it is also essential to focus on retaining your existing customers. Retaining customers is often more cost-effective than acquiring new ones, and loyal customers are more likely to make repeat purchases and recommend your business to others. Use email marketing, loyalty programs, and other strategies to keep your existing customers engaged and loyal to your brand. It is essential to measure your return on investment (ROI) to determine the effectiveness of your advertising campaigns. Use analytics tools to track the costs and revenue associated with each advertising campaign and calculate the ROI for each campaign. Use this information to identify which campaigns are performing well and which ones need improvement. Developing a growth plan and strategy for marketing ads is essential for any business looking to attract customers online and encourage them to make a purchase. By defining your growth goals, analyzing your target market, and developing a marketing plan that includes SEO, PPC advertising, social media marketing, email marketing, and content marketing, you can develop effective advertising campaigns that reach the right audience. By testing and optimizing your campaigns, personalizing your advertising, and focusing on customer retention, you can increase conversions and improve the ROI of your advertising efforts.

# Chapter 7
# Research the Competition to Outperform

Doing research on the competition is an essential part of any business strategy, whether you are operating online or offline. By understanding your competitors, you can identify areas where you can differentiate your business, improve your marketing efforts, and make more money. In this chapter, we will explore some key steps to doing research on the competition for an online business and developing a plan to make more money. The first step in doing research on the competition is to identify your competitors. Who are your main competitors in your industry or niche? Use search engines, social media, and other online resources to identify your competitors and create a list. Once you have identified your competitors, it is important to analyze their websites. Look at their website design, content, and user experience. What are their strengths and weaknesses? Are there any gaps in their offerings that you can fill? Analyzing your competitors' websites can help you to identify areas where you can differentiate your business and improve your online presence. Social media is another important tool for online businesses, and it is essential to analyze your competitors' social media profiles. Look at their follower count, engagement rates, and the type of content they are posting. Are there any social media platforms that your competitors are not using? Are there any opportunities to engage with your target audience on social media that your competitors are missing? Search engine optimization (SEO) is essential for online businesses, and it is important to analyze your competitors' SEO strategies. Look at their keyword research, on-page optimization, and backlink profile. What keywords are they targeting, and how are they incorporating them into their content? Are there any opportunities to target keywords that your competitors are not using? Analyzing your competitors' SEO strategies can help you to improve your own SEO efforts and attract more organic traffic to your website. Pay-per-click (PPC) advertising and social media advertising can be effective tools for online businesses, and it is important to analyze your competitors' advertising strategies. Look at their ad copy, targeting, and calls to action. What advertising platforms are they using, and how are they targeting their ads? Are there any gaps in their advertising campaigns that you can fill? Analyzing your competitors' advertising strategies can help you to develop more effective advertising campaigns and attract more customers. Once you have analyzed your competitors, it is important to develop a differentiation strategy. How can you differentiate your business from your competitors? Are there any gaps in the market that your competitors are not addressing? Can you offer a unique product or service that sets you apart? Developing a differentiation strategy can help you to attract more customers and make more money. Once you have developed a differentiation strategy, it is important to develop a marketing plan that targets your ideal customers. Use the insights that you gained from analyzing your competitors' websites, social media profiles, SEO strategies, and advertising strategies to develop a marketing plan that targets your ideal customers. Consider using a mix of SEO, PPC advertising, social media marketing, email marketing, and content marketing to attract more customers and make more money. To ensure that your marketing campaigns are effective, it is important to test and optimize them on an ongoing basis. A/B testing is a common technique used in digital advertising to test different versions of an ad to see which performs better. By testing different ad copy, images, and calls to action, you can optimize your advertising campaigns to improve performance and increase conversions. Use analytics tools to track your results and make data-driven decisions about how to optimize your marketing campaigns. Some key metrics to track include click-through rates (CTR), conversion rates, and cost per acquisition (CPA). While attracting new customers is important, it is also essential to focus on retaining your existing customers. Retaining customers is often more cost-effective than acquiring new ones, and loyal customers are more likely to make repeat purchases and recommend your business to others. Use email marketing, loyalty programs, and other strategies to keep your existing customers engaged and loyal to your brand. Pricing is a critical factor in the success of any online business, and it is important to offer competitive pricing that is in line with your competitors. Consider offering promotions and discounts to attract new customers and encourage existing customers to make repeat purchases. However, make sure that your promotions and discounts are sustainable and do not negatively impact your profit margins. Customer feedback is an invaluable source of information for online businesses, and it is important to leverage it to make improvements to your business. Encourage customers to leave feedback on your website or social media profiles and use this feedback to make improvements to your products, services, and marketing efforts. Addressing customer feedback can help to improve customer satisfaction and increase loyalty to your brand. Remember to stay up to date with industry trends and developments. Keep an eye on new technologies, changes in consumer behavior, and emerging trends in your industry. Use this information to adapt your marketing strategies and stay ahead of your competitors. Doing research on the competition is essential for any online business looking to make more money. By analyzing your competitors' websites, social media profiles, SEO strategies, and advertising strategies, you can identify areas where you can differentiate your business and improve your marketing efforts. Developing a differentiation strategy, developing a marketing plan, testing and optimizing your marketing campaigns, focusing on customer retention, offering competitive pricing and promotions, leveraging customer feedback, and staying up to date with industry trends are all important steps to making more money and staying ahead of your competitors.

# Chapter 8
# What Google Ads Do for a Business

With Google Ads, businesses can create text, display, and video ads that are displayed on Google search results pages, as well as on other websites and mobile apps that are part of the Google Display Network. So, what exactly does Google Ads do for a business? Here are some key benefits: Reach potential customers when they are searching for your products or services. One of the main benefits of Google Ads is that it allows businesses to reach potential customers when they are actively searching for products or services related to their business. This is because Google Ads uses a pay-per-click (PPC) model, which means that businesses only pay when a user clicks on one of their ads. By targeting keywords related to their business, businesses can ensure that their ads are displayed to potential customers now when they are most likely to make a purchase. Another benefit of Google Ads is that it allows businesses to target specific demographics and interests. For example, businesses can target their ads to users based on their age, gender, location, and interests. This means that businesses can ensure that their ads are displayed to users who are most likely to be interested in their products or services, which can increase the effectiveness of their advertising campaigns. Google Ads allows businesses to control their advertising costs by setting a budget for their campaigns. Businesses can choose how much they want to spend each day, and they only pay when a user clicks on one of their ads. This means that businesses can ensure that they are getting a good return on investment (ROI) for their advertising spend. Google Ads provides businesses with a range of analytics tools that allow them to measure the effectiveness of their advertising campaigns. Businesses can track metrics such as click-through rates, conversion rates, and cost per acquisition, which can help them to optimize their campaigns and improve their ROI. Google Ads also provides businesses with a range of ad formats and targeting options that allow them to create customized campaigns that are tailored to their specific needs. Businesses can create text, display, and video ads, and they can choose from a range of targeting options, such as keywords, demographics, and interests. This means that businesses can create campaigns that are highly targeted and effective. Google Ads allows businesses to reach potential customers across multiple devices, including desktop computers, tablets, and smartphones. This is important because more and more users are accessing the internet on mobile devices, and businesses need to ensure that their ads are displayed to users on all devices. Google Ads can also help to improve a business's search engine optimization (SEO) efforts. By targeting keywords related to their business, businesses can improve their visibility in organic search results, which can increase their website traffic and improve their overall online presence. Google Ads is a powerful advertising platform that provides businesses with a range of benefits, including the ability to reach potential customers when they are actively searching for products or services, target specific demographics and interests, control advertising costs, measure the effectiveness of advertising campaigns, customize ad formats and targeting options, reach potential customers across multiple devices, and improve search engine optimization (SEO) efforts. By using Google Ads, businesses can increase their online visibility, attract more customers, and ultimately, grow their business. Google Ads can be highly effective for small businesses looking to attract new customers and grow their business. With its highly targeted advertising options, customizable ad formats, and cost-effective pricing model, Google Ads provides small businesses with a powerful tool for reaching potential customers and driving sales. One of the key benefits of Google Ads for small businesses is its highly targeted advertising options. Small businesses can use Google Ads to target specific keywords related to their products or services, as well as specific geographic locations and demographic groups. This means that their ads are displayed only to users who are most likely to be interested in their products or services, which can increase the effectiveness of their advertising campaigns. Google Ads uses a pay-per-click (PPC) pricing model, which means that small businesses only pay when a user clicks on one of their ads. This can be highly cost-effective for small businesses with limited advertising budgets, as they can set a daily budget for their campaigns and control their costs. Google Ads also provides businesses with a range of bidding options, allowing them to bid on keywords and set their own maximum cost-per-click (CPC) bids. Google Ads provides small businesses with a range of customizable ad formats, including text, display, and video ads. This allows businesses to create ads that are tailored to their specific needs and preferences, and can help them to stand out from their competitors. Small businesses can also customize the messaging and visuals of their ads to align with their brand identity and target audience. Another key benefit of Google Ads for small businesses is its ability to provide measurable results. Small businesses can use analytics tools to track the performance of their advertising campaigns, including click-through rates (CTR), conversion rates, and cost-per-acquisition (CPA). This allows businesses to make data-driven decisions about their advertising campaigns, and to optimize their campaigns to improve their ROI. Google Ads allows small businesses to advertise across multiple devices, including desktop computers, tablets, and smartphones. This is important because more and more users are accessing the internet on mobile devices, and businesses need to ensure that their ads are displayed to users on all devices. By advertising across multiple devices, small businesses can reach a wider audience and increase their chances of attracting new customers. Google Ads allows small businesses to reach a wider audience than they might be able to through other advertising channels. By advertising on Google search results pages and the Google Display Network, small businesses can reach potential customers who are actively searching for products or services related to their business, as well as users who are browsing websites and mobile apps that are part of the Google Display Network. Finally, Google Ads allows small businesses to compete with larger businesses on a level playing field. Because Google Ads uses a PPC pricing model, small businesses can set a budget for their campaigns and control their costs, which can allow them to compete with larger businesses that have larger advertising budgets. By using targeted advertising options, customizable ad formats, and measurable results, small businesses can create effective advertising campaigns that can help them to grow their business. Google Ads can be highly effective for small businesses looking to attract new customers and grow their business. With its highly targeted advertising options, cost-effective pricing model, customizable ad formats, measurable results, and ability to reach a wider audience, Google Ads provides small businesses with a powerful tool for advertising online. By using Google Ads, small businesses can increase their online visibility, attract more customers, and ultimately, grow their business.

# Chapter 9
# How to Build Your First Marketing Campaign Using Google Ads

Building your first marketing campaign using Google Ads can be intimidating, but it doesn't have to be. With some careful planning and attention to detail, you can create a highly effective marketing campaign that targets your ideal customers and drives sales for your business. In this chapter, we will explore some key steps to building your first marketing campaign using Google Ads. The first step in building your first marketing campaign using Google Ads is to define your goals. What do you want to achieve with your advertising campaign? Do you want to increase website traffic, generate leads, or drive sales? Defining your goals will help you to choose the right keywords, ad formats, and targeting options for your campaign. Once you have defined your goals, the next step is to choose your keywords. Keywords are the words or phrases that users enter Google search when they are looking for products or services related to your business. Choose keywords that are relevant to your business and that are likely to be searched for by your target audience. Google Ads provides businesses with a range of ad formats to choose from, including text ads, display ads, and video ads. Choose the ad format that is most appropriate for your business and your advertising goals. For example, if you want to drive sales, you may want to choose a text ad that includes a strong call-to-action (CTA) and a link to your website. Setting your budget is an important part of building your first marketing campaign using Google Ads. Determine how much you want to spend on your campaign and set a daily budget that aligns with your goals and your advertising budget. Remember that Google Ads uses a pay-per-click (PPC) pricing model, which means that you only pay when a user clicks on one of your ads. Choose the targeting options that are most appropriate for your business and your advertising goals. For example, if you run a local business, you may want to target users who are located within a specific geographic area. Once you have chosen your keywords, ad format, budget, and targeting options, it's time to create your ad. Write compelling ad copy that includes your chosen keywords and a strong call-to-action. Choose a headline that grabs users' attention and a description that highlights the benefits of your products or services. Once you have created your ad, it's time to launch your campaign. Set your bid for your chosen keywords and monitor your campaign closely to ensure that it is performing as expected. Use analytics tools to track your campaign's performance and make data-driven decisions about how to optimize your campaign for better results. To ensure that your marketing campaign using Google Ads is effective, it's important to optimize your campaign on an ongoing basis. Test different ad copy, landing pages, and targeting options to see what works best for your business. Use analytics tools to track your campaign's performance and make data-driven decisions about how to improve your campaign for better results. Finally, it's important to monitor and adjust your campaign on an ongoing basis to ensure that it is meeting your goals and delivering a positive ROI. Use analytics tools to track your campaign's performance, and adjust your budget, targeting, and ad copy as needed to improve your campaign's performance and drive more sales for your business. Building your first marketing campaign using Google Ads can be a powerful way to reach your target audience and drive sales for your business. By defining your goals, choosing your keywords, ad format, budget, targeting options, and creating compelling ad copy, you can create a highly effective marketing campaign that drives results for your business. It's important to monitor your campaign closely, use analytics tools to track your performance, and make data-driven decisions about how to optimize your campaign for better results. By following these key steps and staying focused on your goals, you can build a successful marketing campaign using Google Ads that helps to grow your business and reach new customers. Remember to stay flexible and open to new ideas, as the world of online advertising is constantly evolving, and what works today may not work tomorrow. With the right strategy, however, you can build a strong and sustainable online presence for your business and drive long-term growth and success.

# Chapter 10

# Conversion Tracking and Analytics in Marketing

Conversion tracking and analytics are two critical components of modern marketing strategies. Conversion tracking involves tracking user behavior on a website or application to measure the effectiveness of marketing efforts. Analytics, on the other hand, involves analyzing data collected from tracking and other sources to gain insights into user behavior and improve marketing strategies. Together, conversion tracking and analytics help marketers optimize their campaigns, increase their return on investment (ROI), and ultimately achieve their business goals. Conversion tracking involves tracking user behavior on a website or application to determine the effectiveness of marketing efforts. In general, a "conversion" is any action that a user takes on a website that aligns with a business goal, such as making a purchase, filling out a form, or signing up for a newsletter. Conversion tracking allows marketers to track these actions and measure the success of their marketing campaigns. One common way to track conversions is using tracking pixels or tags. These are small snippets of code that are placed on a website and used to track user behavior. When a user performs a specific action, such as making a purchase, the tracking pixel or tag sends a signal back to the advertising platform, allowing marketers to track the success of their campaigns. Another way to track conversions is using conversion tracking software. This type of software can track user behavior across multiple devices and platforms, providing marketers with a comprehensive view of user behavior and campaign performance. Conversion tracking is particularly important for businesses that rely on online sales or lead generation. By tracking conversions, businesses can measure the effectiveness of their marketing campaigns and make data-driven decisions to optimize their strategies. Analytics involves analyzing data collected from tracking and other sources to gain insights into user behavior and improve marketing strategies. There are many different types of analytics, ranging from simple metrics such as page views and bounce rates to more complex analyses such as user segmentation and predictive modeling. One key aspect of analytics is the ability to measure key performance indicators (KPIs) and track progress towards business goals. KPIs can vary depending on the business and the marketing strategy, but may include metrics such as conversion rates, customer lifetime value, and return on ad spend (ROAS). Another important aspect of analytics is the ability to segment users and analyze user behavior. User segmentation involves grouping users based on common characteristics such as demographics, behavior, and preferences. By analyzing user behavior within each segment, marketers can gain insights into how different types of users interact with their website and marketing campaigns. Predictive modeling is another advanced analytical technique that is becoming increasingly important in marketing. Predictive modeling involves using statistical algorithms and machine learning techniques to analyze data and make predictions about future user behavior. By using predictive modeling, marketers can identify trends and patterns in user behavior, predict which users are most likely to convert, and optimize their campaigns accordingly. There are many benefits to using conversion tracking and analytics in marketing. These benefits include - Improved ROI: By tracking conversions and analyzing user behavior, marketers can identify which campaigns are most effective and allocate resources accordingly. This can lead to improved ROI and a higher return on investment for marketing spend. Data-driven decision making: Conversion tracking and analytics provide marketers with data and insights that can inform their decision-making processes. By making data-driven decisions, marketers can optimize their campaigns and achieve better results. Increased customer satisfaction: By analyzing user behavior, marketers can identify pain points and improve the user experience. This can lead to increased customer satisfaction and loyalty. Better targeting - By segmenting users and analyzing user behavior, marketers can improve their targeting and reach the right users with the right message at the right time. Competitive advantage: Conversion tracking and analytics can provide a competitive advantage by allowing businesses to optimize their marketing strategies and stay ahead of the competition. Conversion tracking and analytics can provide businesses with a competitive advantage by allowing them to optimize their marketing strategies and stay ahead of the competition. Here are a few ways that conversion tracking and analytics can provide a competitive advantage - Optimizing ad spend: By tracking conversions and analyzing user behavior, businesses can identify which marketing channels and campaigns are most effective. This allows them to allocate their marketing budget more effectively, optimizing their ad spend and getting the most value for their money. Targeting the right users: By segmenting users and analyzing user behavior, businesses can identify which types of users are most likely to convert. This allows them to target their marketing efforts more effectively, reaching the right users with the right message at the right time. Improving user experience: By analyzing user behavior, businesses can identify pain points and areas for improvement on their website or application. This can lead to a better user experience, which can increase customer satisfaction and loyalty. Testing and iterating: Conversion tracking and analytics allow businesses to test different marketing strategies and iterate based on the results. This allows them to quickly adapt to changing market conditions and stay ahead of the competition. Predictive modeling: Predictive modeling is an advanced analytical technique that allows businesses to predict future user behavior. By using predictive modeling, businesses can identify trends and patterns in user behavior, predict which users are most likely to convert, and optimize their campaigns accordingly. This can provide a significant competitive advantage by allowing businesses to anticipate market trends and stay ahead of the competition. Overall, conversion tracking and analytics can provide businesses with a competitive advantage by allowing them to optimize their marketing strategies, target the right users, improve the user experience, test, and iterate, and use predictive modeling to stay ahead of the competition. By leveraging the power of conversion tracking and analytics, businesses can increase their ROI, improve their marketing effectiveness, and achieve their business goals.

# Chapter 11
# Bidding Strategies in Marketing to Avoid and Implement

Bidding strategies are an essential part of digital marketing campaigns. They determine how much an advertiser is willing to pay for each click, impression, or conversion on an ad. Bidding strategy can be highly effective in helping businesses reach their marketing goals, but they can also be a source of frustration and wasted budget if not implemented correctly. Let's discuss bidding strategies in marketing, including how to avoid common mistakes and how to implement effective bidding strategies. Manual bidding involves setting bids manually for each keyword or ad group. This approach can be time-consuming and often leads to inefficiencies as it is challenging to manage and optimize many keywords or ad groups. As a result, manual bidding can result in wasted budget and missed opportunities. Overbidding involves setting bids higher than necessary to win auctions. Overbidding can lead to a high cost per click (CPC), which can quickly deplete the advertising budget. Overbidding can also result in wasted clicks from users who are not likely to convert, leading to a low return on investment (ROI). Underbidding: Underbidding involves setting bids lower than necessary to win auctions. Underbidding can result in missed opportunities to reach potential customers, leading to a low impression share and reduced visibility. Underbidding can also lead to a low ad rank, which can negatively impact the quality score and result in a low click-through rate (CTR). Uncontrolled Automated Bidding: Automated bidding is a useful tool that can help advertisers optimize bids based on performance data. However, uncontrolled automated bidding can result in an excessive bid that can quickly deplete the advertising budget. CPC bidding involves setting bids based on the maximum amount an advertiser is willing to pay for each click. CPC bidding is an effective bidding strategy for search engine advertising as it allows advertisers to set maximum bids for each keyword and ad group. CPC bidding can be optimized by adjusting bids based on performance data, such as CTR and conversion rate. Cost per Impression (CPM) bidding involves setting bids based on the maximum amount an advertiser is willing to pay for each impression. CPM bidding is an effective bidding strategy for display advertising as it allows advertisers to reach a large audience while controlling costs. CPM bidding can be optimized by adjusting bids based on performance data, such as viewability and engagement rate. Cost per Action (CPA) bidding involves setting bids based on the maximum amount an advertiser is willing to pay for each conversion. CPA bidding is an effective bidding strategy for campaigns that focus on driving specific actions, such as sign-ups, downloads, or purchases. CPA bidding can be optimized by adjusting bids based on performance data, such as conversion rate and cost per conversion. Enhanced Cost per Click (ECPC) Bidding: ECPC bidding is a type of automated bidding that allows advertisers to adjust bids based on performance data. ECPC bidding can be used for both CPC and CPA bidding strategies and is an effective way to optimize bids based on conversion data. Target Cost per Acquisition (tCPA) bidding is a type of automated bidding that allows advertisers to set a target cost per acquisition. tCPA bidding is an effective bidding strategy for campaigns that focus on driving specific actions and allows advertisers to optimize bids based on the cost per conversion. Set Realistic Goals: Setting realistic goals is essential for effective bidding strategies. Advertisers should understand their marketing goals and the expected ROI before setting bids. Analyze Competitors: Analyzing competitors is crucial for effective bidding strategies. Advertisers should research their competitors and their bidding strategies to gain insights into the market and identify opportunities for optimization. This can help advertisers to adjust their bids and position themselves competitively. Use Performance Data: Using performance data is essential for effective bidding strategies. Advertisers should regularly analyze performance data, such as CTR, conversion rate, and cost per conversion, to optimize their bids and improve their campaigns' overall performance. Segmenting campaigns can help advertisers to optimize bids based on performance data. Advertisers should group campaigns based on themes or performance metrics, such as location or device, to optimize bids and improve the effectiveness of their campaigns. Adjusting bids regularly is essential for effective bidding strategies. Advertisers should adjust their bids based on performance data and changes in the market to ensure that they are getting the most value for their advertising budget. Test Different Bidding Strategies: Testing different bidding strategies is essential for optimizing campaigns. Advertisers should test different bidding strategies, such as CPC, CPM, and CPA, to identify the most effective approach for their business goals. Bidding strategies are an essential part of digital marketing campaigns, and effective implementation can help businesses achieve their marketing goals. Advertisers should avoid common bidding mistakes, such as manual bidding, overbidding, and underbidding, and implement effective bidding strategies, such as CPC, CPM, and CPA bidding. To optimize their bidding strategies, advertisers should set realistic goals, analyze competitors, use performance data, segment campaigns, adjust bids regularly, and test different bidding strategies. By following these tips, advertisers can maximize the effectiveness of their campaigns and achieve their marketing goals.

# Chapter 12
# Keywords and Ads in Marketing

Keywords and ads are essential components of digital marketing campaigns. Keywords are the words or phrases that users type into search engines to find information or products, while ads are the advertisements that businesses use to reach those users. Let's look at keywords and ads in marketing, including how to select the right keywords, how to create effective ads, and how to optimize campaigns for maximum effectiveness. Selecting the right keywords is essential for any digital marketing campaign. Here are some tips for selecting the right keywords - Keyword research is the process of identifying the words or phrases that users are searching for. Advertisers should conduct keyword research to identify relevant keywords for their business, analyze their search volume and competition, and choose the most appropriate keywords to target. Advertisers should focus on user intent when selecting keywords. User intent refers to the reason behind a user's search. Advertisers should select keywords that match the user's intent, such as informational keywords for users looking for information or transactional keywords for users looking to make a purchase. Long-tail keywords are longer and more specific phrases that users use to search for products or services. Advertisers should include long-tail keywords in their campaigns as they are less competitive and more likely to convert. Negative keywords are words or phrases that advertisers can exclude from their campaigns. Advertisers should include negative keywords to avoid irrelevant searches and reduce their advertising costs. Creating effective ads is essential for attracting users and driving conversions. Here are some tips for creating effective ads - Advertisers should use clear and compelling headlines to attract users' attention and encourage them to click on the ad. The headline should be relevant to the user's search query and communicate the value of the product or service. Advertisers should focus on the benefits of the product or service in the ad copy. The ad copy should be relevant to the user's search query and communicate the value of the product or service. Advertisers should include a call-to-action in the ad copy to encourage users to act, such as clicking on the ad or making a purchase. Ad extensions are additional features that can be added to an ad, such as a phone number or a link to the website. Advertisers should use ad extensions to provide users with additional information and increase the effectiveness of their ads. Optimizing campaigns is essential for maximizing the effectiveness of digital marketing campaigns. Here are some tips for optimizing campaigns - Advertisers should track and analyze campaign data to identify areas for improvement and optimize their campaigns. They should use analytics tools to track the performance of their ads, such as click-through rate, conversion rate, and cost per click. A/B Testing: A/B testing is the process of comparing two versions of an ad to determine which is more effective. Advertisers should use A/B testing to test different ad elements, such as headlines, ad copy, and call-to-actions, to identify the most effective approach. Landing pages are the pages on a website where users are directed after clicking on an ad. Advertisers should create landing pages that are relevant to the ad and provide users with the information, they need to make a purchase or act. Quality score is a metric used by search engines to determine the relevance and effectiveness of an ad. Advertisers should focus on improving their quality score by creating relevant ads, selecting relevant keywords, and providing a positive user experience. Here are some tips for improving quality score - Advertisers should create ad copy that is relevant to the user's search query and the keywords being targeted. This includes using the keyword in the headline and ad copy and focusing on the benefits of the product or service. Advertisers should create landing pages that are relevant to the ad and provide a positive user experience. This includes ensuring that the landing page loads quickly, is mobile-friendly, and contains relevant information that matches the user's search intent. Historical performance, such as click-through rate (CTR), conversion rate, and ad relevance, is used by search engines to determine the quality score. Advertisers should focus on improving these metrics by testing different ad elements, refining their targeting, and creating high-quality landing pages. Ad relevance is a measure of how well the ad matches the user's search query. Advertisers should ensure that their ads are relevant to the user's search query and focus on targeting specific keywords or keyword themes to improve ad relevance. Keywords and ads are essential components of digital marketing campaigns. Advertisers should focus on selecting the right keywords, creating effective ads, and optimizing campaigns for maximum effectiveness. This includes conducting keyword research, focusing on user intent, using long-tail keywords and negative keywords, using clear and compelling headlines, focusing on benefit-focused ad copy, including a call-to-action, and using ad extensions. Advertisers should also optimize campaigns by tracking and analyzing data, conducting A/B testing, focusing on landing page experience, and improving quality score. By following these tips, advertisers can create effective campaigns that reach the right users, drive conversions, and achieve their marketing goals.

# Chapter 13
# How to Write Google Ads that Pass Clickthrough Rate

Google Ads are an effective way to reach potential customers and drive conversions. However, the success of a Google Ads campaign depends on many factors, including the quality of the ad copy. Clickthrough rate (CTR) is the ratio of users who click on an ad to the number of times the ad is shown (impressions). CTR is an essential metric for measuring the effectiveness of an ad campaign. A high CTR indicates that the ad is relevant and engaging to the user, while a low CTR indicates that the ad is not resonating with the audience. Knowing your audience is essential for writing effective Google Ads. Advertisers should identify their target audience, including their demographics, interests, and pain points. This information can be used to create ad copy that resonates with the audience and encourages them to take action. Using relevant keywords is crucial for creating effective Google Ads. Advertisers should conduct keyword research to identify the keywords that their target audience is searching for. These keywords should be included in the ad copy, including the headline and ad description, to improve ad relevance and attract clicks. The headline is the first thing that users see when they view an ad. It should be clear and compelling, providing a brief overview of the product or service being offered. The headline should also include the primary keyword to improve ad relevance and attract clicks. Focusing on the benefits of the product or service being offered is essential for creating effective Google Ads. Advertisers should focus on how their product or service can solve the user's pain points and meet their needs. This can be achieved by using benefit-focused ad copy, including the benefits of the product or service in the headline and ad description. Using a call-to-action (CTA) is essential for encouraging users to act, such as clicking on the ad or making a purchase. The CTA should be clear and concise, encouraging users to act, such as "Shop Now," "Sign Up Today," or

"Learn More." Creating multiple ad variations is essential for optimizing Google Ads campaigns. Advertisers should create multiple ad variations, including different headlines and ad descriptions, to test which ad copy is most effective. This can be achieved by using Google Ads' A/B testing feature, which allows advertisers to test different ad variations and optimize their campaigns based on performance data. Ad extensions are additional features that can be added to an ad, such as a phone number or a link to the website. Advertisers should use ad extensions to provide users with additional information and increase the effectiveness of their ads. Ad extensions can also improve ad relevance and attract clicks. Keeping ad copy concise is essential for creating effective Google Ads. Advertisers should keep the ad copy to the point, focusing on the benefits of the product or service and using a clear and compelling headline. The ad description should be brief and easy to read, providing enough information to encourage users to act. Optimizing for mobile is essential for creating effective Google Ads. Mobile devices account for a significant percentage of online searches, and ads that are not optimized for mobile may not display correctly, leading to a low CTR. Advertisers should use responsive design to ensure that their ads display correctly on all devices. Testing and optimizing are essential for creating effective Google Ads. Advertisers should regularly test different ad variations and optimize their campaigns based on performance data. This can be achieved by using Google Ads' A/B testing feature, which allows advertisers to test different ad variations and identify which ad copy is most effective. To optimize campaigns, advertisers should focus on the following metrics - Clickthrough Rate (CTR) is a measure of the number of clicks that an ad receives compared to the number of times it is shown. Advertisers should aim for a high CTR as it indicates that the ad is relevant and engaging to the user. Conversion rate is a measure of the number of users who take a desired action, such as making a purchase or filling out a form, after clicking on an ad. Advertisers should focus on improving conversion rates to drive more conversions and improve ROI. Cost per Click (CPC) is the amount that an advertiser pays each time a user clicks on an ad. Advertisers should focus on reducing CPCs to maximize their advertising budget and improve ROI. Quality Score is a metric used by Google Ads to measure the relevance and effectiveness of an ad. Advertisers should focus on improving quality score by creating relevant ads, selecting relevant keywords, and providing a positive user experience. By regularly testing and optimizing their campaigns, advertisers can improve the effectiveness of their Google Ads and drive more conversions. Writing effective Google Ads that pass clickthrough rate is essential for reaching potential customers and driving conversions. Advertisers should focus on knowing their audience, using relevant keywords, using a clear and compelling headline, focusing on benefits, using a call-to-action, creating multiple ad variations, using ad extensions, keeping ad copy concise, optimizing for mobile, and testing and optimizing their campaigns. By following these tips and focusing on the right metrics, advertisers can create effective Google Ads that drive conversions and achieve their marketing goals.

# Chapter 14
# How to Create Landing Pages in Marketing with Google Ads

Landing pages are an essential component of digital marketing campaigns, particularly for Google Ads campaigns. A landing page is the page on a website where users are directed after clicking on an ad. The purpose of a landing page is to provide users with the information they need to make a purchase or act, such as filling out a form or signing up for a newsletter. Before creating a landing page, it is essential to determine the goal of the landing page. The goal of the landing page should align with the goal of the Google Ads campaign. For example, if the goal of the campaign is to drive sales, the landing page should be designed to encourage users to make a purchase. If the goal of the campaign is to generate leads, the landing page should be designed to encourage users to fill out a form or provide contact information. The landing page should be simple and focused on the goal of the campaign. It should be easy to navigate and provide users with the information they need to make a purchase or act. The landing page should include a clear and compelling headline, benefit-focused ad copy, and a call-to-action that encourages users to act. The landing page should be relevant to the ad that users clicked on. Advertisers should ensure that the landing page content matches the ad content to provide a consistent user experience. This improves ad relevance and increases the likelihood of conversion. The headline is the first thing that users see when they land on the page. It should be clear and compelling, providing a brief overview of the product or service being offered. The headline should also include the primary keyword to improve ad relevance and attract clicks. Focusing on the benefits of the product or service being offered is essential for creating effective landing pages. Advertisers should focus on how their product or service can solve the user's pain points and meet their needs. This can be achieved by using benefit-focused ad copy, including the benefits of the product or service in the headline and ad description. Using a call-to-action (CTA) is essential for encouraging users to act, such as making a purchase or filling out a form. The CTA should be clear and concise, encouraging users to act, such as "Shop Now," "Sign Up Today," or "Learn More." Optimizing for mobile is essential for creating effective landing pages. Mobile devices account for a significant percentage of online searches, and landing pages that are not optimized for mobile may not display correctly, leading to a low conversion rate. Advertisers should use responsive design to ensure that their landing pages display correctly on all devices. Using images and videos is essential for creating effective landing pages. Visual content can help to communicate the value of the product or service and increase engagement. Advertisers should use high-quality images and videos that are relevant to the product or service being offered and communicate the benefits. Testing and optimizing are essential for creating effective landing pages. Advertisers should regularly test different landing page variations and optimize their campaigns based on performance data. This can be achieved by using Google Ads' A/B testing feature, which allows advertisers to test different landing page variations and identify which is most effective. To optimize landing pages, advertisers should focus on the following metrics - Conversion rate is a measure of the number of users who take a desired action, such as making a purchase or filling out a form, after landing on the page. Advertisers should focus on improving conversion rates to drive more conversions and improve ROI. To improve conversion rates, advertisers should focus on the following: Clear and Compelling Call-to-Action - The call-to-action on the landing page should be clear and compelling, encouraging users to act. The CTA should be prominently displayed and easy to find. Simple and Focused Design: The landing page should be simple and focused on the goal of the campaign. The design should be easy to navigate and provide users with the information they need to make a purchase or take action. Benefit-Focused Ad Copy: The ad copy on the landing page should focus on the benefits of the product or service being offered. It should address the user's pain points and demonstrate how the product or service can solve their problems. Relevant Images and Videos: The landing page should use relevant images and videos to communicate the value of the product or service and increase engagement. Advertisers should regularly test different landing page variations and optimize their campaigns based on performance data. This can be achieved by using Google Ads' A/B testing feature, which allows advertisers to test different landing page variations and identify which is most effective. Creating effective landing pages is essential for driving conversions and achieving marketing goals with Google Ads. Advertisers should focus on determining the goal of the landing page, keeping the landing page simple and focused, ensuring landing page relevance, creating a clear and compelling headline, focusing on benefits, using a call-to-action, optimizing for mobile, using images and videos, and testing and optimizing their landing pages. By following these tips and focusing on the right metrics, advertisers can create effective landing pages that drive conversions and achieve their marketing goals.

# Chapter 15

# How to Choose Search Campaigns in Marketing

Search campaigns are a popular and effective way to reach potential customers and drive conversions. Search campaigns are a type of online advertising that allows advertisers to display ads in search engine results pages (SERPs) based on specific keywords. Before choosing search campaigns, it is essential to determine your marketing goals. The goals of your search campaigns should align with your overall marketing goals. For example, if your goal is to increase sales, your search campaigns should be focused on driving conversions. If your goal is to generate leads, your search campaigns should be focused on capturing contact information from potential customers. Keyword research is essential for choosing the right search campaigns. Advertisers should conduct keyword research to identify the keywords that their target audience is searching for. This can be done using tools such as Google Keyword Planner or SEMrush. Advertisers should focus on keywords that are relevant to their business and have high search volume and low competition. Determining your budget is essential for choosing the right search campaigns. Advertisers should determine how much they are willing to spend on their search campaigns and allocate their budget accordingly. It is essential to monitor your budget regularly to ensure that you are getting a good return on investment (ROI). Choosing your target audience is essential for choosing the right search campaigns. Advertisers should identify their target audience, including their demographics, interests, and pain points. This information can be used to create ad copy that resonates with the audience and encourages them to act. Choosing the right ad format is essential for choosing the right search campaigns. Advertisers can choose from different ad formats, including text ads, image ads, and video ads. Text ads are the most common ad format for search campaigns, but other ad formats may be more effective depending on the campaign goals and target audience. Choosing the right bidding strategy is essential for choosing the right search campaigns. Advertisers can choose from different bidding strategies, including cost per click (CPC), cost per thousand impressions (CPM), and cost per action (CPA). The right bidding strategy will depend on the campaign goals and target audience. Monitoring and optimizing your campaigns is essential for achieving your marketing goals with search campaigns. Advertisers should monitor their campaigns regularly, track key performance indicators (KPIs), and adjust as needed. This can be done by using Google Ads' reporting and analytics tools, which allow advertisers to track campaign performance and identify areas for improvement. Choosing the right search campaigns is essential for reaching potential customers and achieving marketing goals. Advertisers should focus on determining their marketing goals, conducting keyword research, determining their budget, choosing their target audience, choosing the right ad format, choosing the right bidding strategy, and monitoring and optimizing their campaigns. By following these tips and focusing on the right metrics, advertisers can create effective search campaigns that drive conversions and achieve their marketing goals. Display advertising is a popular and effective way to reach a large audience and drive conversions. Display advertising allows advertisers to display ads on millions of websites and reach potential customers while they browse the internet. There are several advertising platforms available, including Google Ads, Facebook Ads, and Microsoft Advertising. Each platform has its strengths and weaknesses, and advertisers should choose the platform that aligns with their marketing goals. Determining your target audience is essential for getting ads on millions of websites. Advertisers should identify their target audience, including their demographics, interests, and pain points. This information can be used to create ad copy that resonates with the audience and encourages them to take action. Keyword research is essential for getting ads on millions of websites. Advertisers should conduct keyword research to identify the keywords that their target audience is searching for. This can be done using tools such as Google Keyword Planner or SEMrush. Advertisers should focus on keywords that are relevant to their business and have high search volume and low competition. Creating effective ad copy is essential for getting ads on millions of websites. Advertisers should create ad copy that is clear, concise, and compelling. The ad copy should focus on the benefits of the product or service being offered and include a clear call-to-action that encourages users to act. Choosing the right ad format is essential for getting ads on millions of websites. Advertisers can choose from different ad formats, including text ads, image ads, and video ads. Each ad format has its strengths and weaknesses, and advertisers should choose the format that aligns with their marketing goals and target audience. Setting your budget is essential for getting ads on millions of websites. Advertisers should determine how much they are willing to spend on their display advertising campaigns and allocate their budget accordingly. It is essential to monitor your budget regularly to ensure that you are getting a good return on investment (ROI). Using targeting options is essential for getting ads on millions of websites. Advertising platforms offer several targeting options, including demographic targeting, interest targeting, and behavioral targeting. Advertisers should choose the targeting options that align with their marketing goals and target audience. Using remarketing is essential for getting ads on millions of websites. Remarketing allows advertisers to target users who have previously visited their website or engaged with their brand. This can be an effective way to re-engage users and drive conversions. Monitoring and optimizing your campaigns is essential for getting ads on millions of websites. Advertisers should monitor their campaigns regularly, track key performance indicators (KPIs), and adjust as needed. This can be done by using the reporting and analytics tools offered by the advertising platform. Getting ads on millions of websites is essential for reaching a large audience and driving conversions. Advertisers should focus on choosing the right advertising platform, determining their target audience, conducting keyword research, creating effective ad copy, choosing the right ad format, setting their budget, using targeting options, using remarketing, and monitoring and optimizing their campaigns. By following these tips and focusing on the right metrics, advertisers can create effective display advertising campaigns that reach millions of potential customers and achieve their marketing goals.

# Chapter 16
# How to Build an Audience to Remarket Ads

Remarketing is a powerful digital marketing technique that allows advertisers to target users who have previously interacted with their brand. It is an effective way to re-engage potential customers and drive conversions. However, before you can remarket to an audience, you need to build that audience. The first step in building an audience to remarket to is to install tracking code on your website. Tracking code allows you to track user behavior on your website and capture information about visitors, such as the pages they viewed, the products they clicked on, and the actions they took. This information can be used to build a remarketing audience. The next step in building an audience to remarket to is to determine your target audience. You should identify the specific group of people that you want to target with your remarketing campaigns. This could be people who have abandoned their shopping cart, people who have visited specific pages on your website, or people who have previously made a purchase. Once you have determined your target audience, you can create remarketing lists. Remarketing lists are lists of users who have taken specific actions on your website. For example, you could create a remarketing list of people who have added items to their shopping cart but did not complete their purchase. You can create remarketing lists using the tracking code installed on your website. Another way to build an audience to remarket to is to use customer data. You can use data such as email addresses, phone numbers, or customer IDs to create a remarketing audience. This data can be uploaded to your advertising platform and used to create a custom audience. Lookalike audiences are audiences that are like your existing audience. You can create a lookalike audience based on your existing customer data or remarketing lists. Lookalike audiences can help you reach potential customers who are like your existing customers and may be interested in your products or services. Social media platforms, such as Facebook and Twitter, offer remarketing options that allow you to target users who have previously engaged with your brand on their platforms. You can create a remarketing audience on these platforms using the tracking code installed on your website or by uploading customer data. Google Ads also offers remarketing options that allow you to target users who have previously interacted with your brand on Google's network. You can create a remarketing audience on Google Ads using the tracking code installed on your website or by uploading customer data. Finally, you can use third-party tools to build an audience to remarket to. There are several tools available that can help you build remarketing audiences, such as AdRoll and Criteo. These tools allow you to target users across multiple platforms and networks. Building an audience to remarket to is an essential part of any successful digital marketing campaign. By installing tracking code on your website, determining your target audience, creating remarketing lists, using customer data, using lookalike audiences, using social media, using Google Ads, and using third-party tools, you can build an effective remarketing audience that drives conversions and achieves your marketing goals. By focusing on the right metrics and continuously optimizing your campaigns, you can create effective remarketing campaigns that re-engage potential customers and drive sales.

# Chapter 17
# How to Setup Google Shopping Campaigns

Google Shopping campaigns are a powerful digital marketing tool that allows advertisers to display their products in Google search results. Setting up a Google Shopping campaign can be a complex process, but it is an essential part of any successful e-commerce strategy. The first step in setting up a Google Shopping campaign is to create a Google Merchant Center account. The Merchant Center is where you will upload your product data, manage your product feed, and link your Google Ads account. Once you have created your Merchant Center account, you will need to upload your product feed. Your product feed is a file that contains information about your products, such as the product name, description, price, and image. You can upload your product feed manually or using an automated feed management tool. If you do not already have a Google Ads account, you will need to create one. Your Google Ads account is where you will set up your Google Shopping campaign and manage your ad spend. Link Your Google Merchant Center Account to Your Google Ads Account - Once you have created your Google Ads account, you will need to link it to your Merchant Center account. This will allow you to create and manage your Shopping campaigns from within your Google Ads account. Before you can create your Google Shopping campaign, you will need to set your campaign goals. You should identify the specific goals of your campaign, such as increasing sales or driving website traffic. Google Ads offers two types of Shopping campaigns: standard Shopping campaigns and Smart Shopping campaigns. Standard Shopping campaigns allow you to manually set your bids and manage your campaign. Smart Shopping campaigns use machine learning to automatically optimize your bids and targeting based on your campaign goals. Once you have chosen your campaign type, you will need to choose your targeting options. You can target your ads based on specific keywords, products, or product categories. You can also use audience targeting to target users who have previously interacted with your brand. You will need to set your bid strategy based on your campaign goals. Google Ads offers several bidding strategies, including manual bidding, automated bidding, and enhanced cost-per-click (ECPC). Once you have set your bid strategy, you will need to create your ad groups. Ad groups allow you to organize your products into specific groups based on their category or other criteria. You can create multiple ad groups for your campaign. Finally, you will need to create your ads. Your ads will display in Google search results and will include information about your products, such as the product name, image, and price. You can create multiple ads for each ad group. Setting up a Google Shopping campaign is an essential part of any successful e-commerce strategy. By creating a Merchant Center account, uploading your product feed, creating a Google Ads account, linking your Merchant Center account to your Google Ads account, setting your campaign goals, choosing your campaign type, choosing your targeting options, setting your bid strategy, creating your ad groups, and creating your ads, you can create effective Google Shopping campaigns that drive sales and achieve your marketing goals. By focusing on the right metrics and continuously optimizing your campaigns, you can create successful Google Shopping campaigns that drive revenue and growth for your business. Negative keywords are an essential part of setting up Google Ads campaigns. Negative keywords are the words or phrases that you do not want your ads to appear for. By using negative keywords, you can ensure that your ads are only displayed to users who are likely to be interested in your products or services. The first step in avoiding negative keywords is to research your keywords. Keyword research involves identifying the words and phrases that your potential customers are searching for. By understanding the search intent of your target audience, you can choose the right keywords that will attract potential customers to your website. Broad match modifier keywords are a type of keyword that allows you to control how closely your ads match the user's search query. Broad match modifier keywords include a "+" sign before each word. For example, if you sell women's shoes, you could use the broad match modifier keyword "+women's +shoes". This will ensure that your ads only appear for searches that include the words "women's" and "shoes". Phrase match keywords are another type of keyword that allows you to control how closely your ads match the user's search query. Phrase match keywords include a quotation mark before and after the keyword. For example, if you sell women's shoes, you could use the phrase match keyword "women's shoes". This will ensure that your ads only appear for searches that include the exact phrase "women's shoes". Exact match keywords are the most specific type of keyword. Exact match keywords include the keyword in brackets. For example, if you sell women's shoes, you could use the exact match keyword [women's shoes]. This will ensure that your ads only appear for searches that include the exact phrase "women's shoes" and nothing else. Negative keywords are the words or phrases that you do not want your ads to appear for. Negative keywords can be used to prevent your ads from being displayed to users who are unlikely to be interested in your products or services. For example, if you sell women's shoes, you might want to use negative keywords such as "men's shoes" or "children's shoes". This will ensure that your ads are not displayed to users who are searching for these types of products. Keyword Planner is a free tool provided by Google Ads that allows you to research and analyze keywords. Keyword Planner can help you identify potential negative keywords by showing you the search volume and relevance of different keywords. By using Keyword Planner, you can identify negative keywords that may be affecting the performance of your ads and add them to your negative keyword list. It is essential to monitor your campaigns regularly. By monitoring your campaigns, you can identify any negative keywords that may be affecting the performance of your ads. You can use the search terms report to see which search terms are triggering your ads and identify any negative keywords that need to be added to your negative keyword list. Avoiding negative keywords is an essential part of setting up Google Ads campaigns. By researching your keywords, using broad match modifier keywords, using phrase match keywords, using exact match keywords, using negative keywords, using Keyword Planner, and monitoring your campaigns, you can ensure that your ads are only displayed to users who are likely to be interested in your products or services. By focusing on the right metrics and continuously optimizing your campaigns, you can create effective Google Ads campaigns that drive revenue and growth for your business.

# Chapter 18
# Optimizing Google Ads and Marketing Campaigns

Optimizing your Google Ads campaigns is an essential part of maximizing your return on investment (ROI) and achieving your marketing goals. By continually analyzing and refining your campaigns, you can increase your click-through rates, conversions, and revenue. The first step in optimizing your Google Ads campaigns is to set campaign goals. Your goals will vary depending on the type of campaign you are running, but common goals include increasing sales, driving website traffic, or generating leads. By setting specific and measurable goals, you can track your progress and adjust your campaigns accordingly. The second step in optimizing your Google Ads campaigns is to target the right audience. You can target your ads based on factors such as demographics, location, and interests. By targeting the right audience, you can ensure that your ads are displayed to people who are most likely to be interested in your products or services. Choosing the right keywords is essential for optimizing your Google Ads campaigns. You should choose keywords that are relevant to your products or services and have a high search volume. You can use keyword research tools to identify keywords that are likely to perform well. Once you have identified your keywords, you should group them into ad groups based on their relevance and performance. Writing compelling ad copy is crucial for optimizing your Google Ads campaigns. Your ad copy should be engaging, informative, and relevant to your target audience. You should include a strong call to action that encourages users to click on your ad and act. Testing your ads is an essential part of optimizing your Google Ads campaigns. You can test different variations of your ad copy, headlines, and images to see which performs best. By testing your ads, you can identify what resonates with your target audience and adjust your campaigns accordingly. Ad extensions are additional information that can be added to your ads, such as phone numbers, location, and links to specific pages on your website. Ad extensions can improve the visibility and performance of your ads by providing users with more information about your products or services. Monitoring your campaigns is an essential part of optimizing your Google Ads campaigns. You should regularly review your campaign performance metrics, such as click-through rates, conversions, and cost per click. By monitoring your campaigns, you can identify areas for improvement and adjust your campaigns accordingly. Remarketing is a powerful technique that allows you to target users who have previously interacted with your brand. You can use remarketing to re-engage potential customers who may have abandoned their shopping carts or visited your website but did not make a purchase. Remarketing can help increase your conversions and drive more sales. Conversion tracking is essential for optimizing your Google Ads campaigns. Conversion tracking allows you to track the actions that users take on your website after clicking on your ad, such as making a purchase or filling out a form. By tracking your conversions, you can identify which keywords and ads are generating the most conversions and adjust your campaigns accordingly. Optimizing your Google Ads campaigns is an ongoing process that requires regular monitoring and adjustment. By setting campaign goals, targeting the right audience, choosing the right keywords, writing compelling ad copy, testing your ads, using ad extensions, monitoring your campaigns, using remarketing, and using conversion tracking, you can create effective Google Ads campaigns that drive revenue and growth for your business. By focusing on the right metrics and continuously refining your campaigns, you can maximize your ROI and achieve your marketing goals.

**How to Setup Automated Rules in Google Ads**

Automated rules in Google Ads are a powerful tool that can help advertisers automate routine tasks and adjust their campaigns based on specific criteria. Automated rules allow you to set specific conditions and actions, which will be automatically applied to your campaigns, ad groups, ads, and keywords. The first step in setting up automated rules is to choose the campaign, ad group, ad, or keyword that you want to apply the rule to. You can choose a specific campaign, ad group, ad, or keyword by navigating to the relevant section in your Google Ads account. Click on "Automate" - Once you have selected the campaign, ad group, ad, or keyword that you want to apply the rule to, you should click on the "Automate" button, which is located at the top of the page. Google Ads provides a range of automated rules that you can choose from, including bid adjustments, budget changes, status changes, and scheduling changes. You should choose the type of rule that best fits your needs. Once you have chosen the type of rule you want to create, you will need to set the conditions for the rule. For example, if you are creating a bid adjustment rule, you will need to set the conditions for when the bid should be adjusted. Once you have set the conditions for your rule, you will need to set the action that should be taken when the conditions are met. For example, if you are creating a bid adjustment rule, you will need to set the action for how much the bid should be adjusted. You will need to set the frequency of your rule, which determines how often the rule will be applied. You can choose to apply the rule once, daily, weekly, or monthly. Once you have set up your automated rule, you should review it to ensure that it is set up correctly. You can then save your rule, and it will be automatically applied to your campaign, ad group, ad, or keyword based on the conditions you have set. It is essential to monitor your automated rules regularly and adjust them as needed. You can use the data provided by Google Ads to identify areas for improvement and adjust your rules accordingly. Automated rules in Google Ads are a powerful tool that can help advertisers automate routine tasks and adjust their campaigns based on specific criteria. By choosing the campaign, ad group, ad, or keyword, selecting the type of rule you want to create, setting the conditions and actions for your rule, setting the frequency of your rule, and monitoring and adjusting your rules regularly, you can create effective automated rules that help you maximize your ROI and achieve your marketing goals. By focusing on the right metrics and continually refining your automated rules, you can create successful Google Ads campaigns that drive revenue and growth for your business. Automating and using Google AI in marketing can help businesses improve their marketing strategies and achieve better results. Google AI is a suite of machine learning tools and technologies offered by Google that can help businesses automate tasks, optimize campaigns, and analyze data more efficiently. One of the primary benefits of using Google AI in marketing is the ability to automate repetitive tasks. By automating tasks such as data entry, lead generation, and email marketing, businesses can save time and focus on more strategic tasks. This can help increase productivity and efficiency, allowing businesses to achieve more with fewer resources. Google

AI can also help businesses optimize their ad campaigns by analyzing data and making real-time adjustments. Google Ads, for example, uses machine learning to adjust bids and targeting based on data such as search queries, demographics, and device types. This can help businesses achieve better results and improve their return on investment (ROI) from advertising. Google AI can help businesses personalize their marketing efforts by analyzing customer data and preferences. By using machine learning algorithms to analyze customer behavior, businesses can create targeted marketing campaigns that are more likely to resonate with individual customers. This can help improve the customer experience and increase customer loyalty. Google AI can also help businesses improve their customer service by automating tasks such as chatbots and virtual assistants. Chatbots can provide customers with instant support and answers to their questions, while virtual assistants can help automate routine tasks such as scheduling appointments or making reservations. This can help improve the customer experience and reduce the workload of customer service representatives. Google AI can also help businesses analyze data more efficiently by using machine learning algorithms to identify patterns and trends. By automating data analysis, businesses can save time and gain insights into customer behavior and preferences. This can help businesses make more informed decisions and improve their marketing strategies. Google AI can also help businesses enhance the user experience by using machine learning algorithms to optimize website design and content. By analyzing user behavior and preferences, businesses can create websites that are more intuitive and user-friendly, making it easier for customers to navigate and find the information they need. Automating and using Google AI in marketing can help businesses improve their marketing strategies and achieve better results. By automating repetitive tasks, optimizing ad campaigns, personalizing marketing efforts, improving customer service, analyzing data more efficiently, and enhancing the user experience, businesses can save time, improve efficiency, and achieve their marketing goals. However, it's important to note that Google AI is not a silver bullet and requires careful implementation and ongoing management to achieve the desired results. By investing in the right tools and expertise, businesses can leverage Google AI to drive growth and success in their marketing efforts. Setting up a Gmail campaign in marketing can help businesses reach potential customers directly in their email inbox. Gmail campaigns are part of Google Ads and allow businesses to create ads that appear in the Promotions tab of Gmail users' inboxes. In this article, we will discuss how to set up a Gmail campaign in marketing. The first step in setting up a Gmail campaign is to create a Google Ads account. To do this, go to the Google Ads website and follow the prompts to create an account. Once you have created an account, you will need to set up a billing method and create a campaign. To create a Gmail campaign, navigate to the Google Ads dashboard and click on the "New Campaign" button. Select the "Display Campaign" option, and then select "Gmail Campaign" from the campaign types. Next, choose a campaign goal that aligns with your business objectives. Google Ads offers several campaign goals, including website traffic, leads, and sales. Select the goal that best fits your marketing objectives. After choosing a campaign goal, you will need to set the campaign settings. This includes selecting the geographic location, language, and budget for the campaign. You can also set a start and end date for the campaign. Once you have set the campaign settings, you will need to create ad groups. Ad groups allow you to organize your ads and target specific audiences. For example, you could create ad groups based on customer demographics or interests. After creating ad groups, it's time to create ads for your campaign. Gmail ads are made up of three components: a headline, a description, and an image. You can also add a call-to-action button to encourage users to click on the ad. To ensure that your ads are reaching the right audience, you can target specific demographics, interests, and behaviors. For example, you could target users who have recently searched for products or services related to your business. Next, set a bid strategy for your campaign. This will determine how much you are willing to pay for each click on your ad. Google Ads offers several bid strategies, including cost-per-click (CPC), cost-per-impression (CPM), and cost-per-action (CPA).

After creating your ads and setting your bid strategy, it's time to preview and launch your campaign. Preview your ads to make sure they look and function correctly, and then launch the campaign to start reaching potential customers. Setting up a Gmail campaign in marketing can be an effective way for businesses to reach potential customers directly in their email inbox. By following these steps to create a Google Ads account, set campaign goals and settings, create ad groups and ads, target specific audiences, and set a bid strategy, businesses can launch a successful Gmail campaign and achieve their marketing objectives. As with any marketing campaign, it's important to monitor the performance of the campaign and adjust as needed to ensure that it's achieving the desired results.

# Chapter 19
# How to Use Google Analytics to Track Ad Campaigns

Google Analytics is a powerful tool that allows you to track and analyze your website's performance. By linking your Google Ads account to your Google Analytics account, you can track the performance of your Google Ads campaigns and gain insights into how your campaigns are performing. Link Your Google Ads Account to Your Google Analytics Account - The first step in tracking your ad campaigns in Google Analytics is to link your Google Ads account to your Google Analytics account. To do this, you will need to follow the instructions provided by Google Ads to link your accounts. Once you have linked your accounts, you will need to set up goals in Google Analytics. Goals are specific actions that you want users to take on your website, such as making a purchase or filling out a form. By setting up goals, you can track the performance of your ad campaigns and measure their effectiveness. UTM parameters are tags that you can add to your ad URLs to track the performance of your ads in Google Analytics. By adding UTM parameters to your ad URLs, you can track which ads are generating the most traffic and conversions. You can use tools such as the Google Analytics URL Builder to create UTM parameters for your ads. Once you have set up goals and UTM parameters, you can monitor your campaign performance in Google Analytics. You can use the "Campaigns" report in Google Analytics to track the performance of your ad campaigns. This report provides information on the number of clicks, impressions, click-through rate, and conversions for each campaign. Analyzing your campaign data is an essential part of tracking your ad campaigns in Google Analytics. You can use the data provided by Google Analytics to identify which ad campaigns are performing well and which campaigns need improvement. You can also use the data to identify areas for optimization, such as improving your ad copy or targeting. Google Analytics provides a range of segments that you can use to analyze your campaign data. Segments allow you to filter your data based on specific criteria, such as demographics, location, or device. By using segments, you can gain insights into how different user groups are interacting with your website and adjust your campaigns accordingly. Custom reports allow you to create customized reports that provide insights into your ad campaigns' performance. You can use custom reports to track specific metrics, such as click-through rate or conversion rate, and analyze your data in more detail. Remarketing is a powerful technique that allows you to target users who have previously interacted with your brand. You can use remarketing to re-engage potential customers who may have abandoned their shopping carts or visited your website but did not make a purchase. By using remarketing, you can increase your conversions and drive more sales. Using Google Analytics to track ad campaigns is a powerful way to gain insights into how your campaigns are performing and identify areas for improvement. By linking your Google Ads account to your Google Analytics account, setting up goals, using UTM parameters, monitoring your campaign performance, analyzing your data, using segments, setting up custom reports, and using remarketing, you can create effective Google Ads campaigns that drive revenue and growth for your business. By focusing on the right metrics and continually refining your campaigns, you can maximize your ROI and achieve your marketing goals. Google Tag Manager (GTM) is a tool that allows marketers to manage and deploy marketing and analytics tags on their website without the need for web development skills. It simplifies the process of adding and updating tags to your website, which can save time and reduce the likelihood of errors. What is Google Tag Manager? Google Tag Manager is a free tool offered by Google that enables marketers to manage website tags, or snippets of code that track user behavior and website performance. Website tags can include tracking pixels, conversion tracking, retargeting, and more. Google Tag Manager simplifies the process of adding and managing these tags, allowing marketers to make changes quickly and easily without the need for web development skills.

How to Use Google Tag Manager for Marketing

Set Up a Google Tag Manager Account

The first step in using Google Tag Manager for marketing is to set up a Google Tag Manager account. You can do this by visiting the Google Tag Manager website and following the instructions provided. Once you have set up your Google Tag Manager account, you can create a tag by clicking on the "Tags" tab and then clicking on the "New" button. You can choose from a variety of tag types, including Google Analytics, AdWords, and more. Once you have created your tag, you can add it to your website by clicking on the "Publish" button and selecting the option to "Add Google Tag Manager to your website." You will need to copy and paste the code provided by Google Tag Manager into the head section of your website. It is essential to test your tag to ensure that it is working correctly. You can do this by using the Google Tag Assistant Chrome extension, which allows you to check that your tags are firing correctly and that there are no errors. Triggers and variables allow you to control when your tags fire and what information they capture. Triggers are conditions that determine when a tag is fired, such as when a specific page is loaded or when a specific button is clicked. Variables are pieces of information that can be passed to your tags, such as the current page URL or the value of a specific form field. Google Tag Manager can be used for remarketing, which is a powerful way to re-engage potential customers who have previously interacted with your brand. You can use Google Tag Manager to deploy remarketing tags, which allow you to track user behavior and display targeted ads to users who have previously visited your website. Google Tag Manager can also be used for A/B testing, which allows you to test different versions of your website to see which one performs better. You can use Google Tag Manager to deploy A/B testing tags, which allow you to track user behavior and compare the performance of different versions of your website. Google Tag Manager is a powerful tool that allows marketers to manage website tags without the need for web development skills. By setting up a Google Tag Manager account, creating tags, adding tags to your website, testing your tags, setting up triggers and variables, using Google Tag Manager for remarketing and A/B testing, you can gain valuable insights into your website's performance and optimize your marketing campaigns for better results. By focusing on the right metrics and continually refining your tags and campaigns, you can maximize your ROI and achieve your marketing goals.

# Chapter 20
# Outsourcing Marketing Agency

Hiring a Google Ad agency can be a great way to optimize your online advertising campaigns and improve your return on investment (ROI). However, it's essential to do your research and choose the right agency for your needs. Before hiring a Google Ad agency, you should have a clear understanding of your business goals and what you hope to achieve through online advertising. You should be able to articulate your target audience, budget, and expected ROI. Having a clear understanding of your goals will help you to evaluate potential agencies and ensure that they are a good fit for your needs. When evaluating potential Google Ad agencies, you should look for relevant experience in your industry or niche. Ideally, the agency should have experience working with businesses like yours and have a proven track record of success. Ask for case studies or examples of previous campaigns they have run and look for evidence of measurable results. Different Google Ad agencies may have different approaches to online advertising, and it's essential to evaluate their approach to ensure that it aligns with your business goals. Look for agencies that take a data-driven approach to advertising and use testing and optimization to improve results. Ask about their process for keyword research, ad creation, and targeting to ensure that they are using best practices. Reporting is an essential part of any online advertising campaign, and it's crucial to understand how an agency will report on the performance of your campaigns. Look for agencies that provide regular and transparent reporting, including metrics such as click-through rate (CTR), conversion rate, and cost per acquisition (CPA). Make sure that the agency is willing to provide regular updates and answer any questions you may have. Good customer service is critical when working with a Google Ad agency. Look for agencies that are responsive to your needs and provide timely and effective communication. Make sure that they have a dedicated account manager who will be your point of contact and who can provide regular updates on your campaigns' performance. Pricing is an important consideration when hiring a Google Ad agency, and it's essential to understand how the agency will charge for their services. Look for agencies that offer transparent and competitive pricing, and make sure that there are no hidden fees or charges. Ask about their billing cycle and how they will charge for services such as campaign setup, ongoing management, and reporting. Hiring a Google Ad agency can be a great way to optimize your online advertising campaigns and improve your ROI. However, it's essential to do your research and choose the right agency for your needs. By understanding your business goals, looking for relevant experience, evaluating their approach, understanding their reporting process, considering their customer service, and evaluating their pricing, you can choose the right agency and achieve success with your online advertising campaigns. Outsourcing marketing campaigns can be a great way to leverage the expertise and resources of external agencies to achieve better results. However, it's important to be aware of potential warning signs before outsourcing to ensure that you select the right agency for your needs. One of the most significant warning signs when outsourcing marketing campaigns is a lack of transparency. If an agency is not transparent about their processes, pricing, or reporting, it can be challenging to evaluate the effectiveness of their campaigns. Look for agencies that are open and transparent about their approach and are willing to provide regular updates and reporting. Another warning sign is a lack of relevant experience. When outsourcing marketing campaigns, you want to work with an agency that has experience working with businesses like yours and has a track record of success. Ask for case studies or references and look for evidence of measurable results. Beware of agencies that overpromise results. While it's important to set ambitious goals for your campaigns, it's also essential to be realistic about what can be achieved. Look for agencies that are transparent about the expected results and are willing to work collaboratively with you to achieve your goals. Communication is key when outsourcing marketing campaigns, and poor communication can be a significant warning sign. Look for agencies that are responsive to your needs and provide timely and effective communication. Make sure that they have a dedicated account manager who will be your point of contact and who can provide regular updates on your campaigns' performance. A lack of creativity can be a warning sign when outsourcing marketing campaigns. Look for agencies that are willing to think outside the box and develop innovative solutions that will help you to stand out from the competition. Make sure that they are not relying on standard templates or cookie-cutter solutions. High turnover rate can be a warning sign when outsourcing marketing campaigns. If an agency has a high turnover rate, it can indicate that they are not providing a positive work environment for their employees. This can lead to a lack of continuity and consistency in your campaigns. Outsourcing marketing campaigns can be a great way to achieve better results, but it's important to be aware of potential warning signs before outsourcing. Watch out for lack of transparency, lack of relevant experience, overpromising results, poor communication, lack of creativity, and high turnover rate. By being vigilant and doing your research, you can select the right agency for your needs and achieve success with your marketing campaigns.

# Conclusion

Google My Business (GMB) and Google Ads are both products offered by Google to help businesses improve their online presence and reach more customers. However, they are not the same product and serve different purposes. What is Google My Business? Google My Business is a free tool offered by Google that allows businesses to manage their online presence across Google, including Google Search and Google Maps. With Google My Business, businesses can create a business profile, add photos, respond to customer reviews, and update business information such as hours of operation and contact information. Google My Business is designed to help businesses connect with local customers and improve their local SEO. By creating a business profile on Google My Business, businesses can appear in Google Maps searches and in the local pack, a set of three local business listings that appear at the top of Google search results. Google Ads (formerly known as Google AdWords) is an advertising platform offered by Google that allows businesses to create and run ads on Google and its partner websites. With Google Ads, businesses can target specific keywords and audiences, set a budget, and create text, image, or video ads. Google Ads is designed to help businesses reach potential customers who are actively searching for their products or services. Ads can appear at the top of Google search results, on partner websites, and in other Google products such as YouTube and Gmail. Google My Business is primarily designed to help businesses manage their online presence and improve their local SEO, while Google Ads is designed to help businesses reach potential customers through targeted advertising. Google My Business is free to use, while Google Ads requires a budget to run ads. Google My Business listings appear in Google Maps searches and the local pack, while Google Ads appear at the top of Google search results, on partner websites, and in other Google products. Google My Business does not allow businesses to target specific keywords or audiences, while Google Ads allows businesses to target specific keywords, demographics, locations, and more. Google My Business does not offer advertising formats, while Google Ads offers a variety of ad formats, including text, image, and video ads. Google My Business can help businesses improve their local SEO and attract more local customers, while Google Ads can help businesses reach a broader audience and achieve a higher ROI through targeted advertising. Google My Business and Google Ads are two different products offered by Google that serve different purposes. While Google My Business is designed to help businesses manage their online presence and improve their local SEO, Google Ads is designed to help businesses reach potential customers through targeted advertising. By understanding the differences between these two products, businesses can make informed decisions about how to optimize their online presence and reach more customers. Marketing is a crucial aspect of any business, regardless of its size. Small businesses can benefit greatly from effective marketing strategies that can help increase brand awareness, generate leads, and boost sales. The first and most important purpose of marketing for small businesses is to build brand awareness. A strong brand can help differentiate your business from competitors and make it more memorable to potential customers. By developing a strong brand identity and promoting it through marketing channels such as social media, email marketing, and content marketing, small businesses can increase their visibility and attract more customers. Marketing can also help small businesses generate leads by identifying and targeting potential customers. By creating targeted marketing campaigns that focus on specific customer segments, small businesses can attract more qualified leads and increase the chances of converting them into paying customers. Effective lead generation strategies may include email marketing, social media advertising, and search engine optimization (SEO). Another purpose of marketing for small businesses is to increase sales. Effective marketing strategies can help businesses reach more customers and convince them to purchase their products or services. By developing compelling messaging, creating a sense of urgency, and offering promotions or discounts, small businesses can encourage customers to make a purchase and increase sales. Marketing can also help small businesses establish trust and credibility with potential customers. By sharing customer testimonials, awards, or industry recognition, small businesses can demonstrate their expertise and reliability. This can help build trust and confidence in potential customers, making them more likely to choose your business over competitors. Marketing can also help small businesses expand their reach beyond their local market. By leveraging digital marketing channels such as social media, email marketing, and SEO, small businesses can reach customers in other geographic locations and expand their customer base. This can be particularly useful for businesses that offer products or services that can be delivered digitally or shipped. Marketing can help small businesses build long-term customer relationships by engaging with them on a regular basis. By providing valuable content, responding to customer inquiries and feedback, and offering exclusive promotions, small businesses can encourage customer loyalty and repeat business. This can help increase the lifetime value of each customer and contribute to the long-term success of the business. Marketing is a critical component of the success of any small business. By building brand awareness, generating leads, increasing sales, establishing trust and credibility, expanding business reach, and building long-term customer relationships, small businesses can increase their visibility and attract more customers. Effective marketing strategies may include a combination of digital marketing channels, such as social media, email marketing, SEO, and content marketing. By investing in marketing and developing effective strategies, small businesses can achieve their goals and drive growth for their business.